THE
HOMEFRONT CLUB

THE
HOMEFRONT CLUB

THE HARDHEADED WOMAN'S GUIDE TO RAISING A MILITARY FAMILY

JACEY ECKHART

NAVAL INSTITUTE PRESS
Annapolis, Maryland

Naval Institute Press
291 Wood Road
Annapolis, MD 21402

Library of Congress Cataloging-in-Publication Data
Eckhart, Jacey, 1965–
The homefront club : the hardheaded woman's guide to raising a military family / Jacey Eckhart.
    p. cm.
Includes bibliographical references.
ISBN 1-59114-228-8 (alk. paper)
1. Families of military personnel—United States. 2. United States—Armed Forces—Military life. 3. Military spouses—United States. 4. Women and the military. I. Title.

UB403.E27 2005

Printed in the United States of America on acid-free paper ∞

12 11 10 09 08 07 06 05   9 8 7 6 5 4 3

Contents

To Brad—
Worth it.

THE
HOMEFRONT CLUB

Introduction

Killing Richard Gere

THERE ARE DAYS WHEN I think about strangling Richard Gere—especially when I consider that classic final scene from *An Officer and a Gentleman*. You remember it. Gere strides manfully into the paper bag factory and sweeps Debra Winger off her feet. She soul kisses him; puts his cover on her head. They march out to tumultuous applause, sun glistening off his fabulous white uniform.

It's quite a scene, but it's nothing compared to the way the story usually plays out in real life. The real-life military bride gets swept up by her man in uniform too. She looks back over his broad shoulder to see her applauding family (who may be glad just to be rid of her). She looks ahead to a glamorous future (to be played out in California or Europe or, say, Guam).

Just as she snuggles up to his chest, thinking she's been rescued from her less-than-idyllic life, His Gorgeousness slams the factory door with the heel of his

1

shiny shoe, sets the bride down on her own two feet, and makes her walk the rest of the way.

It's a shocker. Let me tell you. No wonder Richard Gere does not sleep well at night. But as shocking as it may be, as difficult as military life may appear, many of us find that this real-life scene actually is the beginning of Happily Ever After.

But it is *just* the beginning. They forget to mention that in the movie. Instead, we watch the happy movie couple leave the factory and assume that they, at least, enjoy wedded bliss. They never get assigned to a backwoods town with no jobs or schools or friends for spouses. They always have enough money to buy Diet Coke. And all the little Gere babies arrive in a timely, planned, affordable manner.

In real life, that never, never, *never* happens. We marry into the military and the thrill ride begins—without a safety harness. At first, Love Alone does sustain us. But then we discover that the military guy's hours are ridiculous. He always seems to have the duty on weekends. He doesn't get paid nearly what he is worth. He totes the command's bad mood home with him like a seabag of swamp socks.

And we well-meaning, intelligent, bodacious brides—we are so alone.

Suddenly, the brass buttons don't look quite so shiny any more. In the round of daily life, we military wives start to get the idea that this Man-in-Uniform thing wasn't such a good idea. We start seeing moms at the clinic sniping at their kids and realize where the term "military brat" came from. We run into chicks whose husbands are deployed acting as if they have passed over the Line of Forgetfulness. We notice that some of the senior officers' wives wear a bitter look like they've been chewing coffee beans for twenty-two years. Is this really the life we signed up for?

Would Debra Winger Put Up with This?

Maybe not. Those Hollywood types are not really known for their stamina. But in this situation, you have a sneaking suspicion that even Debra Winger would hang around if she were waiting for *your* husband.

Your husband is a great guy. He has his flaws, sure, but you have this feeling that if you can't be married to him, you can't be married to anyone. You love him, right down to the sound of his carburetor chugging in the driveway. You're starting to hate the military, though. Or perhaps you already hate it with a passion that makes your eyes roll back into your head—and stick.

It is at this eye-rollin' moment in your life that you know you have to do *something*. You've considered throwing violent, Technicolor projectile-vomiting fits. You've thought of developing a rare, non-fatal disease that requires a quiet civilian life with your beloved at your side. You've even considered marching up to the White House to get a signed note from the Commander in Chief saying the world is officially at peace and your husband's presence is no longer required.

That may work. Sure. You try it. Because if you can't figure out a way to convince your beloved to get out of the military, or if he isn't one of those guys who spontaneously comes up with this idea on his own, you're going to have to develop another life plan. You're going to have to either get rid of your guy (uh-oh) or figure out how to live peacefully with the military. You have to discover the secrets to living the Happy Military Life.

Which sounds like an oxymoron, I know. "Happy" and "military" do not frequently appear in the same sentence. But people, even people you know, do manage to make it happen.

Look a little harder at the clinic and the commissary and the command picnic. There are husbands and wives associated with every single service who are genuinely happy with their military-spouse life. They are committed to the military community. They love the excitement of change. They enjoy the pomp and circumstance. They treasure whatever it is in their spouses that makes them want to serve their country.

They must be possessed.

Or not. Maybe they are just ordinary people who have learned to school their thoughts in a way that makes the demands of the military no more important than the weather. Sometimes the sun shines on their parade. Sometimes the rain ruins their picnic. Sometimes they get orders to the same duty station as their Best Friend of All Time. Sometimes they realize their spouse has been out of town since approximately 1992.

It doesn't matter. Because their spouses, their kids, and the principles that rule their lives are actually bigger than anything the military can dish out.

How a Nice Girl Like Me Ended Up on a Post Like This

It isn't just me. Seems like everyone in this country loves a man in uniform. No mystery there. Our guys are spiffy. They're burly. They're duly employed. Even the women in uniform look pretty darn good. Our soldiers, sailors, airmen, Coasties, and Marines put on their hats every day and deliver freedom boxed up like a pizza. I *love* those guys.

But I did not intend to marry one. Growing up on an Air Force base, I always planned to be one of those women capable of loving men in uniform from afar—very, very afar. Intimate with the joys of multiple moves and dads not home for Christmas, I thought I'd be better off as a civilian. I'd be delighted to pay my taxes and admire military guys from the safety of a house that never altered, from a neighborhood that never changed. Stultifying suburbia was the goal.

I didn't make it. When I was all of twenty years old, I went to a Navy football game in Indiana with my parents, sat next to the only man in uniform I'd ever date, and fell in love.

My father, a fighter pilot with twenty-five years in the service, took note. He observed that Brad actually understood what I was talking about most of the time. Held my hand in public. Kissed my grandmother. It was hopeless. But I was Daddy's little girl and he was my dad. My *military* dad.

So when I headed back to college that winter, Dad tapped on the windshield and motioned for me to roll down my window. The most taciturn of men, he bent to look in my upturned face. "Daughter, your mother and I think Brad is a fine, upstanding young man. We like him." He paused; my mother nodded.

"But, honey," he said gently, "the life he offers you . . ." He fumbled for the right word. "The life he offers you *sucks.*"

Sucks? My mother and I looked at each other. We didn't even know he knew that word. But I was grown up. I paid my own rent. I'd read a pile of romance novels.

"Oh, Daddy," I burbled, "I love him. I know all about the military. And six months with him is better than a whole lifetime without him!"

I looked up at my father and glowed. The way only a child can glow. My father patted my arm and turned away from the car. Six months later he patted my arm again as he gave me away to a man in uniform. And every year after that he wordlessly patted my arm as my husband left on five different deployments, as my young family moved to Japan, and as I delivered our third child while Brad was at sea.

As is so often the case between fathers and daughters, we were both right. My husband is a fine, upstanding young man. Six months with him is better than a lifetime without him. And, not to put too fine a point on it, the life he offers me inside the military *sucks*.

I Mean That in the Nicest Way

When I say the military life sucks, I do mean that in the nicest way. The military needs service members to train in the field and at sea and in skies all over the world. Thus, servicemen and servicewomen must be mobile by definition. We stalwart souls who marry into the military (as well as our children, our hamsters, and our basketball hoops) must be just as mobile, just as self-sufficient.

Sometimes that sucks.

Among military wives of the past, even expressing such a sentiment was taboo. Good wives kept a stiff and smiling upper lip. When my mother was a young military wife, she was expected to attend teas, live on base, and refrain from wearing curlers at the commissary.

By the time I married into the military, all of that had changed. Spouses were no longer even mentioned on fitness reports—which is, of course, how it should be. But when the military axed the close supervision of wives, the societal supports that used to bridge the gap for young military families collapsed. When the command stopped paying attention, we families stopped attending all those keep-'em-busy-and-out-of-our-hair activities. We stopped meeting and knowing and supporting each other. These days, families sink or families swim, and they do it alone.

Out Here on Our Own

When my husband deployed for the first time, I was, like most young military brides, set down alone in Nowhere, USA, and expected to go to it. Find a house. Find a job. Make myself happy. Except no one was helping; no one was even watching.

The ship had a support group—but only scary people attended. I had military friends—but none of them had any more experience than I did. We didn't know if it was normal for a twenty-three-year-old to sleep with the lights on. Or whether a baby would fail to bond with a dad who was gone all the time. Or if loneliness could be cured with a two-pound bag of Twizzlers.

In my mother's day, military wives would pass on basic knowledge to one another over bridge games and tennis matches and Red Cross meetings. Since we didn't have those activities, my friends and I had no one to ask our most important question: Could you live happily ever after in the military, or were you crazy even to try?

We looked for guidance. The family service centers on base offered brightly colored sheets of "tips" for deployment. We did not do "tips."

Books aimed at military families delved into the mysteries of rank, pay stubs, and place settings for formal dinners. No military families we knew ever attended anything more formal than a backyard barbecue.

Magazine and newspaper articles featured miraculous military families who seemed to volunteer at the same rate that corporate attorneys reported billable hours. We didn't even have time to sort socks.

The literature was certainly available if you only wanted to know *what* you were supposed to do. But when it came to being a reasonably happy military family, no one told you *how*. And perhaps, more importantly, no one told you *why*. Why should you wait for a man who professes to love you while he disappears for six months at a time? Why should you attend family support-group meetings when you are already so busy? Why should you move to another state or another country when your whole life is running so smoothly right here?

When I couldn't find answers anywhere else, I started writing a column for a base magazine, then a newsletter. Three years later, my newspaper column, "The Homefront," was picked up by the *Virginian-Pilot* in Norfolk, Virginia, home of the largest military installation in the world. Not only was the column a job, it was a way for me to write myself out of the mess I had gotten myself into.

In the column, I explored *how* and I explored *why*. Sometimes I ranted in print; sometimes I whined. Sometimes the column read like the literal equivalent of nine packs of Equal. Sorry about that.

But despite my inadequacies, my readers—active duty, long retired, and even civilian—and I taught each other some amazing things. We found that our happiness is in our own hands, with or without the military. We found that acknowledging the difficulties of this life, laughing at them, and loving—*really* loving—that man in uniform are the best ways to reach that happiness.

Join the Club

Perhaps the most important thing we discovered when we tried to spell out the secrets of happy military families is that there actually are such things. There are happy military families, and they have their trade secrets.

These aren't the kind of secrets that people keep to share with an exclusive group, the kind you have to be deemed worthy to earn. The trade secrets of happy military families are the kind of secrets we forget to tell one another, forget to list, forget to enumerate. By the time we learn them, they are second nature. We can't imagine that anyone else does not know them. They are our admission to the club.

For we are all in a club—the Homefront Club. Without ever signing up, without ever paying dues, without ever electing a leader, we have joined the generations of daring women before us who married the military. We do not join because we have to. We do not join because we are weak young things mewling that our marriage left us with no other choices. It's the twenty-first century. We always have choices.

We join the Homefront Club partly out of strength and partly out of desperation. We join because we know we have chosen a life so different from other people's lives. We join because we are willing to think, really *think,* about the best way to live, the right way to live, and to act on that all the time—even when we don't feel like it.

Living and thinking like civilian people simply isn't possible when you are married to the military. You can't live within babysitting distance of your parents. You can't plant a tree on the day your child is born and expect to watch them grow up together. You can't follow the well-worn patterns of the people you grew up with. Trying to be civilian when you're not is guaranteed to make you crazy.

And we aren't crazy. Instead, we find ourselves in a Homefront Club comprised mostly of women. I know that we refer to each other correctly as "spouses." Men are sprinkled among us, but their experiences being married to female service members are so different from our experiences that those guys must have their own secrets. They are welcome in our club, but not everything that applies to us applies to them.

For husbands or wives, joining the Homefront Club is about being willing to forge a new path. To go with the flow. To catch the bounce pass and go in for a layup. More than likely, you were already that kind of person before you married into the military. Or you wanted to be. The fact that your life was going to be different from other people's lives sounded good to you. You just didn't expect it to be so darn hard.

Nor did you expect to be so lucky. Because we are lucky to have chosen the breadth of a military life. We are lucky to be married to the kind of people drawn to serve in the military. We are lucky to recognize the moment we say yes to the rest of our lives.

Inner Peace Does Not Happen Overnight

I'd love to tell you that some fabulous, metamorphic inner peace about Living Military takes over the very moment you join the Homefront Club. I'd love to give you a things-to-do list for achieving Happy Family-hood. I'd love to tell you that you will read this book (or just buy it) and the very next day your heart will be healed and you'll feel all happy all the time. Hurray for moving? Hurray for sleeping alone when Creepy Pot-Smoking Guy lives across the street? Hurray for not being able to make it to your own sister's baby shower?

Unfortunately, I can't tell you that inner peace comes overnight or that it comes so easily. But I can welcome you to the Homefront Club. I can share some of the trade secrets I've learned in my thirty-eight years as an Air Force brat, seventeen years as a Navy wife, fourteen years as the mom of three military kids, and eight years as a military-life columnist.

The secrets I've learned won't miraculously turn your military life into a day at the beach. But they will show you how to be one of those military spouses who aren't beating their heads against the tarmac every time their service member deploys. Like them, you are going to resolve to see your life more clearly. You are going to try to understand what motivates your husband. You are going to actively seek out happy military families to emulate. You are going to take responsibility for your own happiness (which probably means that strangling Richard Gere is out).

Marriage ebbs and flows. Problems surface and fall away. Irritations flare up and then recede. Military marriage isn't easy. But if you know in your heart of hearts that this is the right guy for you, you can learn how to do it. It is a skill to be learned, a craft to be mastered, not a God-given talent that some people have and some people don't.

Knowledge is power. The learning curve is steep. We are all in this together. Welcome to the Homefront Club.

1

Ten True Things About a Man in Uniform

RESEARCHERS ARE ALWAYS STUDYING our men and women in uniform as if they were a bunch of extremely jaunty lab rats. They study their skin, their teeth, their reflexes. They worry about their exposure to chemicals and the reliability of their safety equipment.

These scientists have discovered our service members are more politically conservative than the average American. They are more likely to believe in God. Their hair is shorter, of course. Most of them prefer tradition, methodical planning, logical decision making, blah, blah, blah, blah.

Are there any studies that make it easier to understand the guy whose plastic shoes are cluttering my closet?

Instead of the scientific stuff you can pick up elsewhere, I'm listing here my highly unscientific observations about the Men in Uniform I have known, loved, and fed over the past thirty-eight years.

1. He Is Not Your Average Joe

Billy Crystal and Debra Winger (her again?) made a movie called *Forget Paris*. Everybody forgot it, except me. Crystal plays a referee for the NBA who meets Winger in France. They fall in love and she moves back to the States to marry him. His travel schedule (ah ha!) brings them to the brink of divorce; she begs him to quit.

It could have been my family—except for the France and NBA part. The year I saw that movie, Brad's travel schedule kept him away from home 87 percent of the time. It meant I could only talk to him by phone on Christmas Day. It meant I kept our one-year-old strapped in his high chair so he wouldn't take his first steps without his daddy present. I was begging Brad to quit the service, calling headhunters, and circling power ties in catalogues.

Then I saw this movie. In one scene, another referee pulls Billy Crystal aside at a barbeque. This referee tells him about a friend who dumped his first wife because she didn't understand how important his job was to him. "If you're with a woman who doesn't get it," the referee advises Crystal, "if she doesn't get what you're about, what's in your guts—move on."

Move on? Is understanding a man's work really that important? It is in the military. You aren't required to understand his taste for pork rinds or his fondness for all things Minnesota Viking, but you do have to understand his work. You have to understand what it is about this work that feeds him. I didn't get that until I saw the movie.

I looked around my neighborhood. The military life was clearly not feeding everybody. Lots of average Joes were finishing their tours and getting out—despite the bad economy. Not my husband.

I could see on a daily basis the exact price Brad was paying to work this job. Having little bitty kids will do that to you. I could see the missed bath times, the beards made of soap bubbles, the silly singing. The gradual development of new words and new routines. How could anyone miss that on purpose?

No one keeps a military job just for the safe and steady paycheck. No amount of money would make it worthwhile to be so far away, in so much danger, and missing so much at home.

But when I look at this man I married, I see a person who is not an average Joe. He is the kind of man who would be tortured by the idea

The Window

"If I join up, honey, will you come with me?" It seems military guys have a window in their careers for marriage. Why else would so many marriages get started right before boot camp? Or right before the first duty station? Or immediately upon news of an overseas tour? Are these big, strong guys afraid to go on their little adventures alone?

A few do seem to glom on to whichever woman they can grab at the time—women as old as their mothers, women with multiple children from multiple fathers, women they've known for a period too short to allow milk to expire.

Marriage is an awfully big step to take just because a guy doesn't want to go home to an empty apartment. That doesn't explain the phenomenon. I think the explanation is that PCS (Permanent Change of Station) moves and deployments have a way of creating long-distance relationships. A couple learns early whether this is Always and Forever or All the Girls I've Loved Before.

Were you, in essence, issued along with the seabag? Then consider yourself lucky, and start working with your husband right now so your marriage will outlast his first set of uniforms.

of being safe in the suburbs while others were doing Something Real. He is the kind whose heart needs an adventure, whose hands need to be in contact with a ship or a plane or a tank, whose lungs can not adequately expand and fill inside an office cubicle.

Is that your husband too? Then you've got problems. Because the person you are married to has joined the ranks of service members who are Doing What They Are. Understand that. They aren't *being* whatever it is that they do, like the rest of us. They are doing exactly What They Are.

That doesn't mean our men feel jolly when they're being shot at in 125-degree heat. Or they aren't miserable when their cruise is extended. Or they don't wish they could go home and bask, doglike, under a big AC. But their feelings about the hardships of deployment and the pain of separation aren't going to last once they get home. They aren't going to remember exactly how many nights they went to bed pining for you. They aren't going to remember what they smelled like after living without hot water for six months. You will, maybe, but they won't. Call it selective amnesia.

After your service member has been home awhile, he will get Cascade-ed and Colgate-ed and Armor All-ed and Cheeto-ed to his heart's content. He will stand around at a back-to-school night like every other guy. Then someone will ask if he was Over There with that certain note of interest and awe.

Hear those words and look right at him. Then let your heart freeze and your feet stand still because you, young woman, are married to a Soldier, a Marine, a Sailor, an Airman, or a Coastie.

You can set your back against it and holler all you want. But if you stay with him, deployments, separations, and war will be a part of your married life. And it will be OK. I promise. Because some time after you accept him for who he is and where he is and what he does, it all gets a little easier. I don't know how it happens, but it does.

2. He Can't Rescue You

Maybe the white uniform and the new car convinced me that my military boyfriend was a Knight in Shining Armor. Until I married him, I wasn't even aware I wanted (much less needed) rescuing. But I must have. Why else would I have thought it was normal to sit on our bed and cry to my newlywed husband, "Why can't you make me happy?"

This happened more than once, I fear. Don't tell my mom. "Oh, honey," I remember him sighing on one occasion (I think he had been working a fifty-seven-hour shift). "I don't know why I can't make you happy. I'm really, really trying."

Of course he was trying. That's the one thing these military guys will do. These are the kinds of guys who feel a personal responsibility to fix everything—even the stuff inside your head. They will try to rescue you from your messed-up family. They will swear they can prevent you from feeling lonely ever again. They will even attempt to slay your self-esteem/chunky-thigh issues. And if all else fails, they will kiss you and try to make it all better. Where do we find these fabulous guys?

But no matter how well meaning they are, no matter how hard they try, they can't defy the laws of nature. They can't make you happy. They can't rescue you from yourself. That's your job.

It bites, I know. There have been days, weeks, months, even years when I would have liked to have let down my golden hair and been rescued from this ridiculous tower. That, sadly, was not to be. You have to climb your own hair. Which is fine.

Learning to Rescue Yourself

The minute you get used to making yourself happy, you learn that rescuing yourself is up to you as well. Just as being married to a cop or a fireman is supposed to make a woman feel safer, being married to a military guy makes you think he will protect you. And he will. When he's there.

The problem is, he's gone quite a lot. Especially during hurricanes, typhoons, earthquakes, raging wildfires, towering infernos, all other natural disasters—and pretty much whenever else you need him. This man who is pledged to protect and serve his country isn't necessarily going to be around to protect and serve you. Because 287 million other people get to come first.

You watch the unit dash off or the boat pull away from the pier, and you're left alone to tape the windows and evacuate the kids. His disappearing act leaves you feeling not only unsafe, unprotected, and uncherished—but angry too.

I think that's why all hurricanes are named after military spouses.

Even a strong woman wants to feel cherished, protected, and maybe even rescued Rapunzel style. It does happen from time to time. But marriage doesn't make you a glorified child, a pampered pet. Marriage makes you a wife, a grown-up by definition. Recognize that rescuing and protecting you 24/7 isn't one of your husband's responsibilities. It's yours. And it can be the making of you.

3. He Can Love You and Still Leave You

One night after I had been married for about ten years, I stood outside a sushi restaurant with Kathleen. On our way to the cars, we starting discussing what Kathleen and her husband, Andrew, planned to do if they had a baby the following year.

"I don't know," I said thoughtlessly, my mind stuck on their hectic schedules. "I just don't understand how people can expect to leave an infant in day care for ten hours a day."

"What Andrew and I don't understand is how Brad can leave his wife and kids for six months at a time," Kathleen retorted.

I stopped dead for a second, then walked on with her, continuing the day care debate as if I hadn't heard. With every step, her question stung me.

How can a man who professes to love his wife and kids as much as Brad does agree to leave them for six months of deployment?

Why doesn't he quit the Navy if he really loves me?

How can you call this love?

To most people, our military marriages must look like too much work. We live far from the help of our extended families. We move all the time. We certainly aren't rich. And then our husbands leave us alone for days, weeks, and months at a time—even when we're stationed overseas.

"Most people have turned their solutions toward what is easy and toward the easiest side of the easy," wrote the poet Rainer Maria Rilke. "But it is clear that we must trust in what is difficult; everything alive trusts in it." In our military marriage, Brad and I have both come to trust in the difficult. It's been our only option. The military has a way of trying and testing a young marriage before it has been made strong. Our first two deployments nearly broke us up. They pointed out in painful detail just where our characters were cracked and flawed. They showed us where we were still unformed, where we weren't really strong enough to conquer the deployment. Yet.

Over the next few years, we did what so many military couples have done before us, what Rilke calls "the difficult work of love." Brad encouraged and praised my efforts to finish school and to find work, friends, and hobbies. I listened to him talk about his job and tried to get to know the cast of characters. He learned to fashion a ponytail on our three-year-old daughter. We slowly, slowly deepened our understanding of what love is and how much it can do.

What used to be love as simple addition has now progressed through subtraction, multiplication, and long, long, looooong division. Our marriage is now in the shallowest pools of geometry, anticipating the depths of trigonometry, calculus, and differential equations yet to come.

How can he love you if he leaves you?

Kathleen's question, one that we military wives have asked ourselves a thousand times, is the question of a beginner just starting the difficult work of love. You don't explain geometry to first graders. You hand them crayons to draw a red circle, a blue square, a green triangle. Each new lesson builds on the previous one. Start here: A man can love his family and still work at a job that requires him to leave them. You do the math.

4. He Can Be an Excellent Father and Husband

I have it on best authority (my refrigerator repairman) that a man who wants a family ought to leave the military. "You can't be a good dad and be in the service," says Fridge Guy, who served his first tour and got out. "You're away all the time and you miss everything. And the divorce rate in the military is way higher than anywhere else in the world."

This is gospel truth to him, but not to me. Being in the military is not an automatic good-fatherhood disqualifier. Being in the military doesn't make a guy the Great Santini. Plenty of military men are excellent husbands and exemplary fathers—perhaps better than they would be outside the military.

I may be a little biased. To start with, my own father served for twenty-five years in the Air Force. Dad gave us the typical military life, moving his wife and family fourteen times. He was flying in Vietnam when my brother was born in Cincinnati. When I was five years old, he missed Halloween because he was on alert. But he wired the tail onto my leopard costume before he left so it would stick straight up and wave as I walked. Fridge Guy might call my dad an absent father, but my family would not. He was not gone "all the time." He did not miss "everything." For mercy's sake, the man sewed my prom dress. Throughout our lives, my siblings and I have benefited from being the children of a devoted husband, a responsible father, a military man. My brothers, my brother-in-law, our many friends, and my own husband merely confirm my original belief.

Bob's Law of Averages

Perhaps Fridge Guy does have a point when it comes to the military and divorce. When you see a slew of marriages break up in your command, especially following a deployment, it's hard to ignore those statistics showing that 25 percent of married couples get divorced in the first seven years. It's hard not to notice that 77 percent of people in the military are under thirty-five years old. And it seems logical to assume that the younger you are, the more likely it is that your marriage will fail.

But age and inexperience are not the only factors that put a marriage at risk. The truth is, the military does stress marriages in a way that civilian life does not.

Our friend Bob, a submarine captain, has seen a lot of divorces pass across his desk. He has a theory we call Bob's Law of Averages.

"Some marriages are perfect going in," says Bob. "Nothing the military will throw at them will be able to break them up. Some marriages are terrible. No matter what happens, these people will divorce. But it is in the average marriage that the military makes the most difference."

Will a deployment, an illness, or a bad move hit the marriage at its most vulnerable moment? You don't know going in. In an average marriage, though, careful thought, earnest communication, and some good therapy can counterbalance the hardships the military throws at you. In the average marriage, attitude is everything.

5. He Will Never Be Rich

While Operation Enduring Freedom was taking place, the media reported that the average family of a 9/11 victim would be entitled to $1.6 million in compensation from the federal government. The family of the average soldier who died in

Is He Worth It?

Before you take another step, you need to ask yourself one thing: Is He Worth It?

Some men are not. I mean that. Some men are not worth waiting for, not worth following, not worth one more second of your precious life.

Putting on a uniform doesn't make a man good husband/father material. It doesn't make him truthful. It doesn't make him brave. A uniform doesn't make a mean man kind or a weak man strong.

Don't be fooled by badges, brass, and buttons. Some of the scariest people I have ever met were in uniform. These men were probably admirable combatants; great in a firefight. But they were not particularly good people to entrust with a tender body or soul.

There is nothing easy about military life. But it's worth it for a worthy man. One who is kind, loving, hardworking, responsible. You can't commit yourself or your children to a life like this for anyone less— especially for any man who has ever pushed you, hit you, beaten you, drawn blood.

Trust in this. The stress of military life will only bring more of the same. And, if you stay with a man who hurts your babies, you are worse than a fool. You must be able to depend on this man and he must be able to depend on you, or you will never make it.

A book can't help you manage a man who is abusive, alcoholic, or addicted. You can't make him a better person just by wishing that he were. If you do find yourself in an abusive situation, be aware that the military offers many, many forms of help. Please look into them. You deserve it.

Afghanistan would receive his Service Members Group Life Insurance benefit of $250,000. Ironic, isn't it?

The difference in scale seemed to appall the media—they who measure the worth of everything in dollars. The soldiers they interviewed didn't seem very upset, though. For one thing, these military guys were planning on winning, not dying. Also, they knew they weren't in the military for the money.

No one enters the military planning to get rich. It offers a secure paycheck and good benefits. It's a way to finance college. Sometimes there is a bonus or two (we're still waiting—hint, hint). And the retirement is decent compared with what you find in the civilian world.

Like teachers, writers, musicians, and cops, our service member is doing what he loves. He is fulfilling his destiny. We're lucky that our guys don't offer to do the job for free. Which is darn wonderful when you think about it. You just can't let yourself think about it when your ATM card gives up for dead at the commissary. You can't think about it when you're losing closing costs on yet another home. You can't think about it while you're working as a minimum-wage slave to pay your student loans or to buy socks.

While we are delighted that our men are doing so well at their work, we military spouses would like them to get paid what they are worth. Which this country could not afford.

Cleansing breath, ladies. Hoo. Hoo. Hoo. Hoo. Heeeeeeeeeeeeeeeee.

My best friend says her irritation over her husband's paycheck isn't with her all the time—anymore. But it does lurk under the surface like a fever blister, flaring up under stress, clearing up later, leaving not a mark. The money virus is always there. Don't let it interfere with your real life.

6. He Will Make You Green with Envy

It was a singularly undignified day. My daughter's teacher scolded me for entering the building before school hours. A woman in a green Blazer rolled down her window and screamed at me. A skinny man in a shiny shirt, riding a bicycle that cost more than I pay in federal taxes, snarled at me to pick one side of the path or the other.

Considering the grinding minutiae of my life, is it any wonder I envied those guys sleeping in the mud in Iraq? Or the ones sailing in circles in the Arabian Sea? Everything about the war in Iraq made my life seem unbearably small. I was embedded with people whose blood pressure shot up over school rules, morning traffic, bike paths. The guys in Iraq were not. While I crawled up the interstate behind thirty SUVs, they were in convoys of tanks plowing through the desert. While I passed out oranges and little bags of chips to lacrosse players, they were holding back crowds desperate for blankets, food, and water. While I skidded across Matchbox cars in my darkened house, they wore night-vision goggles and fought their way into hospitals to rescue fallen comrades. No man left behind. Except me.

I have felt this way before. Not only when the troops were actively engaged in battle, but when they rescued boat people. Or stopped drug traffickers. Or made a port visit in Italy, Venezuela, or Thailand. They were doing something so real. I was scrambling eggs.

My friends and I confess to this envy even when the events are happening to strangers. When it's our own husbands, we are even more bothered.

I am haunted by a scene from the movie *Forrest Gump*. Moments after Forrest and Bubba arrive in Vietnam and join their company, a hundred helicopters swoop over the bay in the background. A hundred helicopters. Nothing I do will ever warrant the presence of a hundred helicopters. Nothing I will ever do will warrant even one—unless I run into that lady in the Blazer again.

An argument could be made that what we do at home is the reason our guys are over there. That *this* is Real Life. That spending ten minutes on the floor with my toddler as he watches the light shine through the mini-blinds is the most important work in the world. But does it compare to liberating a country? Deposing a dictator?

I am safe, and that is a good thing. I wouldn't want to be in danger. I wouldn't want to be living in Baghdad or trying desperately to get out. I wouldn't want to live without electricity or running water. I am more grateful than you know for the remarkable safety of living in the United States.

But being safe is not living large. Whatever these soldiers and airmen and Marines suffer in their military service, for the rest of their lives they will have done something, been someone.

While they are doing the job, our troops will be scared, tired, bored, wet. Things they've never heard of will grow between their toes. Their friends will die. They will become old men and women with damp eyes on Memorial Day, thinking of unbearably young people they used to know. They will dream bad dreams.

And I will be an old woman too. I will forget how the forsythia bloomed in April, how the snow came down in January. I will forget the dishes I stacked in the dishwasher and how my son settled himself in my lap.

Our troops won't forget. They won't ever forget this part of their lives. Or the swooping of a hundred helicopters.

7. He Has No Idea if He's Staying in or Getting Out

You'd think such a strong, motivated, intelligent guy would have a plan when it came to his career. Think again. Your husband could be moaning and groaning about the job every day for four years, counting the milliseconds between him and the outside world. Then, with no warning, he'll come home one day and announce he's reenlisted. Or taken new orders—the kind that require an eight-year commitment. It's enough to make a normal woman do her own brain surgery.

We saints at home can understand why our beloved entered the service. For centuries, men have joined the military as a respectable way to escape the limited circle of home, family, backwater town—even if the town is as big as Brooklyn. Others join because they are sick of working three jobs to make ends meet. Or they want to make something of themselves. Still others enlist as a way to pay for school, or to put off school until they're ready to settle down to a real job. Most like the idea of serving their country. They want to have an adventure. Fine.

But when their tours are up, how do they decide to stay in or get out? Don't look for a grand plan. Because each career decision hinges on the previous one. Sometimes they don't even know this is true. All they see is the path right at their feet. They like their particular job or hate it.

They're good or bad at the work they're doing. They feel rewarded or tortured. Their family is handling it or falling apart. They respect their boss and want to be like him or her, or they think the boss is Captain Queeg incarnate.

Generally, service members stay in or get out according to the circumstances of the moment. Sometimes, though, they reenlist for other reasons. Senior military people seem to understand these decisions. Get a group of them together and they'll give you a host of explanations for why men stay in the military. They are looking for the fathers they never had. They want to know how to be men. They want to do work that is clearly men's work. (Women do this work too, but they have their own reasons.) They like being part of the military community. They like the benefits, the active lifestyle, the athleticism, the bonuses, the retirement, the security, the whole idea of being a protector and a provider. They stay in for their buddies.

So what will make them get out? All service members eventually get to the point in their careers when they have to decide if the benefits outweigh the costs. Only then will some decide they are ready to test the waters on the outside.

8. He Must Be Faithful to You

Add adulterers to the list of men who are not worth waiting for. Separations are too frequent in military life to worry that your spouse is cheating on you. To my way of thinking, faithfulness is a given. What else can you say? It's the cover charge, the starting gun, the bare minimum required. Without it, all bets are off, all contracts null and void.

Back home, we spousal units live up to our end of the bargain. We feed the dog, stuff math facts into the kids, and turn the ignition on that silly truck once a week so some kind of wacky ring will be lubricated. We have earned our husbands' respect—a respect that should be demonstrated by physical fidelity at the very least. We count on it, we deserve it, we expect it. Just as they expect to come home to find that we've been utterly faithful—despite the fact that we are the ones living in a Target Rich Environment.

Happy military families can't function on anything less than perfect faithfulness. Military guys know that. But do they also know that we spouses at home expect fidelity from the whole military community?

Even though adultery may be common in the rest of the world, and expected in certain military branches, we spouses want *everyone* to refrain. Because no matter how unlikely it is that a cheating spouse will be caught, it does happen, and it affects the whole community. People remember how others act. The niggling doubt that someone could betray the one person closest to him in the world changes how his fellow service members view him. If he can lie to and cheat on his wife at home, can he be completely trusted at work?

The military is not a group of superhuman individuals. It's made up of people, flawed and weak, just like all human beings. Service members do not earn our respect by being perfect, but by trying to live their lives in the most honorable way possible. And surely, what shows up on the battlefield begins at home.

9. He'll Be Your Ally against All Comers

In her book *The Shelter of Each Other,* psychologist Mary Pipher recalls a tale about frogs. If you toss a frog into a boiling beaker, the frog will save itself by instantly leaping out. But if you put the frog in a beaker of cool water and then heat it slowly, the frog will stay in the water and die. The frog will adapt to the change in temperature without noticing that it has reached dangerous levels.

I don't know if this is true. I am not habitually cruel to frogs. But Pipher says that the modern family has a lot in common with frogs. In the past, all the hot water we got into came from the outside: war, pestilence, disease, hunger. We banded together to leap out as fast and as far as our frog legs could carry us. In the modern family, however, most of the things threatening us are slowly happening on the inside. Degree by degree, we don't eat meals together. We tag team at the kids' soccer games and music lessons. We watch 267 channels at once. We are more intimate with virtual strangers on the Internet than we are with the people sitting on our couch. We fall asleep next to each other without saying a word. We allow ourselves to live separate lives. The military changes that. Once you are a military family, the worst things that happen to you once again come from the outside: war, injury, separation, cross-country moves.

You can blame your husband and his silly career for bringing these troubles into your life, or the two of you can band together. Us against them. You and me against the world. Making the conscious decision to work together will give you the power you need to make it through.

10. He Won't Appreciate You—Yet

When it comes to understanding what my husband is thinking, we are definitely on the Five-Year Plan. It goes something like this. Five full years after an important event—proposal of marriage, birth of child, purchase of minivan—he will suddenly announce his true thoughts, motivations, and feelings about the incident.

We know neither the day nor the hour that this blessed event will occur; we are just grateful for its occurrence.

Evidently, this happens all over the military. It happened in my town when a group of veterans decided to put up a replica of a statue called "The Homecoming" in our local park. The statue was nice enough— seven feet of cast bronze depicting a first-class petty officer embracing his wife, their son flinging his arms around the couple. The original, located at the Navy Memorial in Washington, D.C., makes women turn away in tears. For us, there is something too poignant in this little group. Too raw. Too reminiscent of harsh edges we've rubbed smooth with time.

But the group erecting the statue was made up of men, not women. Older men, retired from the military years ago. Men who built other careers, other lives. The organizers reported that some of the donors accompanied their checks with letters about patient wives, tender children, faces on a pier caught in wind and snow and rain.

I don't understand why men can only describe these things years after the fact. Is there something about age that makes men understand what it means to have someone waiting at the end of the pier? Someone who missed you? Someone who couldn't wait to welcome you home?

It seems like something they would want to talk about *now*—the way you looked, how you acted, what you wore. How much it all mattered.

But they don't.

At least the young ones don't. They are so engulfed in the heady business of Making a Living and Getting Ahead that they don't have the time to think it all through. Until later. Later they will speak. Sometimes with words. And sometimes with statues.

2 Your Place in His Career

How to Out-Cleaver June Cleaver without Even Trying

LET ME ASK YOU SOMETHING. Does your husband feel *he* has a place in *your* career? I didn't think so. Merciful heavens, that phrase "your place in his career" must be the silliest string of five words ever slung together and taken seriously. Your place in *his* career, indeed. Who are you supposed to be? Mamie Eisenhower in hip-huggers?

But the military is really, really weird. You knew that already. Whether you were hoping for the invitation or not, the military does set a place at the table for the spouses, children, and parents of service members. Shoot, some ex-wives are still hanging around.

Marry into the military, be born into the military, donate your nearest and dearest child to the military, and you're in. Just like that, you've got a place in his career. One big, happy family. Dive right into the soggy nachos.

However, there is a downside to all this happy-happy-joy-joy. You may be part of the family, and certainly welcome to the free health care and commissary privileges if you have an ID card, but you aren't considered a full-blooded member of the tribe. Even if you are a member of the Homefront Club. Unless you personally are wearing the uniform, you are not a ranking relation of the family and will not be treated like one.

This may be a relief to you. You can wear your own flattering clothes and shoes that match your skirt. You won't develop the same psychoses the regular family members pass among themselves. Be thankful for that, at least.

I've found that the secret to fitting into the military family, without actually enlisting, is to consider yourself an in-law. The lovely bride who happened to stumble into this mess. The fine young woman who promises to love, honor, and bring a covered dish to all upcoming events.

You will be a person the military family wants to please, just as your real in-laws want to please you. You will be someone who adds joyfully to the original mix. But most of the time, you won't have to be a vital member of the mission. Relax. That's his job, not yours.

Whatever Happened to Military Wives?

At one time, the military looked carefully—perhaps too carefully—at its spouses. Little blurbs would show up on a husband's fitness report about his wife's suitability, her zest for being a team player, the speeding ticket she got for going nineteen in a fifteen-mile-an-hour zone. Kudos would be thrown to good wives who contributed to the command (i.e., the ones who raised the most money).

Then, in the late seventies, they dropped it. The military no longer mentioned wives on fitness reports. They dropped it completely from the agenda—as if the requirement had never existed.

We are women, not fools. Since our presence was no longer requested in writing, we spouses began to slink away from Army functions and Navy balls and Marine Corps parties. We were filled with relief to be free from that constraining mold and vowed never to look back.

And yet, some of the old competitive pressure seems to have lingered. When I go to military parties and command functions, I sometimes see women cleavering each other, slicing off all the bits that aren't exactly Military Wife. They still act as if there's a mold we must fill, like we're still playing the game, still entering the competition.

I remember an all-military party a few years back, when the conversation among the wives focused on "My Husband's Brilliant Career," "Our Children Are All Gifted," and "I'm the Busy-Bee Lady—Much Busier Than You." Why do the husbands of female service members never have these conversations?

One woman actually cornered me three times to mention (sotto voce) that her babysitter was the daughter of a *Rear Admiral*.

I carefully looked over my shoulder. Nope. No judges present for the Queen Military Wife contest. Woo, boy. I don't have heels that go with this swimsuit. In fact, I don't have heels to go with *any* swimsuit.

This is a club. Not a competition. I cannot say that strongly enough. In these days of military cuts, cost overruns, and nation building, the military has no time to worry about whether or not some guy's wife is adding to his career. They aren't flashing your picture up at the advancement boards. They aren't thinking about you.

The competition between military spouses is over. We all won. You are now free to be your true self. As long as social services doesn't have to come to your house to get your kids. As long as you pay your bills. As long as you avoid substance abuse. As long as your behavior does not prevent the command from getting the job done.

Sure, there are still a few June Cleavers around, lurking behind a platter of handmade puff-pastry tartlets. But there are more of us—many more—than there are of them. Thankfully, that particular military-wife model is just about extinct.

So please come back to the parties. Come back to the Hail and Farewells. Come back to the Family Support Group and the Family Readiness Group. You can sit next to me. I've got a thousand questions about the Harley-Davidson you're restoring in your garage. I'm interested in which Regency Romance novelist you think is best. I want to know where you got your shih tzu and how you manage your career as a welder/ballerina.

Come back, military wife. Honestly, I'm dying to meet you.

I'm Not Your Average Military Wife

So why aren't you interested in being part of this fabulous military community (aside from all the times you've been cleavered)? I can hear your answer. "Because I'm not your average military wife."

Neither am I. Neither is anyone. The one thing military spouses have in common (aside from a certain fatal weakness) is that we all feel as if we don't quite fit in—because we don't. Not one of us qualifies as the average military wife. We're too young or too old. Better educated, not as educated. We are of different cultures, different religions, different politics. There are even liberals and vegetarians sprinkled among us, like so much lovely parsley.

Even when it comes to our children, none of us is the same. We military spouses are blessed with children, happy without children, desperately wishing for children. Desperately wishing aforementioned children had an on/off switch surgically implanted in the backs of their squirrelly little heads.

This feeling of being an outsider is particularly hard on wives who really *are* atypical, especially older women and those married to limited-duty and warrant officers. It's hard to feel like one of the crowd when you and your husband are considerably older (and blessedly more experienced) than other couples in grade. What fun it must be to find that your oldest kid and the nearest ensign have the same CD collection, played at the same decibel level. What a joy to notice that the tech working alongside your spouse still has time to take care of her mane of naturally red hair. And she thinks we're interested in her frizz problems. Ugh.

When we don't feel comfortable in the embrace of the military family, it is awfully tempting to turn away. To drop out. To air kiss.

Don't do it. Those people who all look alike on the outside—the same age, the same clothes, the same cars—have the same thing in common with you. They feel like they don't fit in. It's simply a matter of degree.

The Growth and Development of the Military Spouse

A young spouse has run into her husband's commanding officer in line at the movie theater/commissary/package store/wherever. As we tune in, Commanding Officer has smoothly congratulated Young Spouse on the new assignment her service member just received.

"It's great," says the spouse slowly. "But it does mean another move for the family. That makes eight moves in ten years."

Ding! Ding! Ding! Danger, Will Robinson! Danger!

Question: Is this spouse about to

a. ask the CO to call the detailer and fix it so her True Love never has to move again?

b. demand that the CO come over and move her couch during his leisure minutes?

c. do nothing—she's going through a stage?

d. drop off her children and divorce papers on the quarterdeck the morning the ship deploys?

Did you pick "c"? No? Remember this is my quiz. When in doubt, I always pick "c." Especially when it comes to dealing with the military spouse.

Over the course of True Love, this spouse works toward accepting the demands of the military the way other people accept a climate where it rains every weekend, or a magnolia-ringed yard that will not grow grass, or a box of Popsicles that never has a red one. This takes time—years even.

In your unit, you will see spouses at every one of the following stages. You have to completely finish one stage to move on to the next. Enlisted? Officer? Once again, it doesn't matter. Everybody has to slog through the same stuff. What stage are you in?

Excitement. The first stage of our relationship with the military is marked by white lace and promises. When speaking about the military, new spouses are most likely to mention universal health care or earning a degree. They are sure they'll get assignments in Europe! Or California! Or, say, Guam! These spouses are often overheard promising their mothers that Chuck's whole career can be done right here in San Diego. Let's buy a house!

Abject Fear. This stage emerges the moment the spouse is looking down the throat of the first deployment and realizes she is strapped in for the duration of the ride. AAAAgh! The spouse, who was perfectly capable of turning off her bedroom lamp in her own apartment before her marriage, now hears strange sounds. The presence of an alarm system, hermetically sealed doors, and a dog the size of an SUV does not significantly affect this fear. The best sign of this stage is the late-night phone calls in which the spouse cries, "I didn't think it was going to be like this!"

Denial. This stage usually takes place during the first shore tour or training command. "We aren't going to have to do that again," the spouse tells her friends. The end of this stage generally occurs when the soldier comes home and announces he's reenlisted and his unit deploys on Thursday.

Anger. At the eight-to-ten-year point, the spouse probably has a couple of kids in the bathtub screaming at 146 decibels, "I want my daaadeeeee." She has eaten macaroni and cheese until it is hanging from her ears, like some really wacky jewelry. The car in the driveway has a mysterious ailment that even the most expensive mechanics can't figure out.

At this stage, she is most likely to receive a phone call from the Bahamas where That Marine is out drinking mai tais on the beach and smoking a stogie. Luckily, he is too far away to have his eyebrows completely plucked off. During these years, she will enumerate how many times she's given birth without him, how many times she's moved without him, how she is never going to finish school or get off the night shift, and how there is *still time* to get out of the Marine Corps.

Acceptance. How does this happen? It is a miraculous event rivaled only by the powers of yeast to make bread. Some of us resign ourselves to it as if it were a twenty-year prison sentence. No bigee. I can stand on my head for twenty years. Others just wake up one morning and feel fine about living in the Air Force. Really. They can totally manage this, no problem. Until they accidentally slip back into one of those other stages. I tend to teeter off into the anger stage every time I fret over the price of real estate.

The biggest problem with this stage is that those who attain it only have a hazy recollection of ever having been in any of those other stages. This is the stage in which you are most likely to hurt that younger spouse with an unrealistic recollection of how easy and fun it all was. Remember the truth, ladies. And share it.

Embracement. I was going to drop my discussion of stages at the acceptance point. I had no idea there was any more to aspire to. But my mentor, Char Foley, reminds me there is another stage: embracement. "Most people don't get here," says Char. "This is where you realize that you are truly part of the Something Bigger than you are. You are giving back to your country. You see the big picture. When you meet people who embrace the military, you want to be like them."

This is a stage that a couple comes to together, or not at all. As much as you see your spouse's contribution to the military, he must see yours. Embracing the military brings contentment to the marriage, security to the family, peace to the workplace. I sure hope I can get there from here.

Now I'd like to add a second question to my quiz, and ask that commanding officer to take it.

Question: You hear the warning bells of complaint from that same young spouse. Your first inclination is to shrug and say, "It's an adventure." Instead, you

c. exclaim, "Wow! Eight moves. That's a lot for the Air Force."

c. use the opening to say how this job is going to help her husband's Army career.

c. explain that some jobs in the Coast Guard move more often than others.

c. describe how the Marine Corps depends on spouses, especially during a move.

c. ask a little more about her situation. Show that in the big scheme of Navy life, she matters.

Remember, it's my test. Pick "c." Always pick "c"—for compassion.

Mandatory Fun

Outside the military world, spouses also have a place in each other's careers. I once read a letter in Dear Abby about the husband of a personnel recruiter who didn't want to attend his wife's twice-yearly business socials. He said he was bored and felt dumb. He said she didn't pay enough attention to him during these events.

Abby told the recruiter to let the poor man stay home and just tell people that her husband had (nudge, nudge, wink, wink) "other plans." In the following weeks, civilian couples wrote in to brag that they were so liberated they never attended each other's business events. Others said that the modern woman isn't required to be attached to her husband at the hip.

Please.

I think we are missing the point here. I hate to tell those boss types, but no spouse really wants to attend the mandatory fun. We've got to get a sitter. We have to wear funny shoes. The food is hard to eat while standing. And, frankly, we're all shy.

I'm not sure how this new nonattendance attitude is affecting the business world. In the military community, it's a bad seed taking root. We spouses feel free to skip the picnics and pass on weddings. We have "other plans" the night of the deployment brief—unless they are taking attendance. Then we grumble a lot. Or at least I do. Maybe I should stop that.

Regardless, there is something about going to your spouse's work event that makes you feel like the bouffant hairdo and the big can of hairspray can't be far behind. And that's just if you're a guy.

Why go? Because we have that darn relationship to the command that you simply don't get on the civilian side. It's weird. I can't explain it. It has just sort of evolved, like an extra appendix or double belly buttons.

So what's in it for us besides the lumpia and the roast pig sandwich?

We look silly staying home. Whether we like it or not, everyone we work with knows who's married and who isn't. Could be that whole gold ring thing. Men think if they attend their wife's event, it looks like they're being dragged around by an eyebrow ring. Women think if they go to their husband's event, it looks like they have nothing better to do than discuss the merits of Huggies versus Pampers. Believe me, no one thinks that much about your political leanings. Go to the event and check the box.

It will build your character. For most of our lives we toddle along feeling just great. We've got jobs. Our kids say "please" and "thank you." We don't lock our keys in the car more than twice a year. My, my we are full of ourselves, aren't we? Taste the humility of standing in a group of people laughing at a story you do not understand. Stand alone while your spouse runs off for "a second" to get you a drink. Watch the hands of the clock move backwards with impunity. It's character building. Now go say hi to someone who looks more miserable than you. She may know where they're hiding the smoked salmon.

You'll get to know the cast. When your spouse deploys, the first e-mails and phone calls are all about you. How you are doing? How's the checkbook? Did you finally find those socks? But after a few weeks, the messages home are all about the USS *Floating High School* your spouse lives on. If you haven't attended the picnics and parties, you have no clue that Jennifer is six feet four inches tall and can take care of herself. That the sergeant who throws stuff weighs about eleven pounds less than you do. That Don and Juan are the last sailors in the world you would expect to speak fluent Arabic.

They'll get to know you. It's hard to listen to a guy complain that his wife doesn't understand him when you were right there at the Christmas party lookin' all bright-eyed, bushy-tailed, and In Love With Him. Granted, the entire concept is enough to make Gloria Steinem sick. If you do it, he'll get the rolled eyes from his buddies that he deserves—but not if the unit has never met you.

You don't have to win a beauty contest. Leave concerns about being overweight, underdressed, shy, and possessed of a particularly virulent zit for me to worry about. Any spouse loyal enough to show up at one of these events deserves a shiny gold star next to her name and a Lexus in the driveway. You are a couple. Reflect well on each other.

You could meet a new friend. I met my best friend, Dawn, at a ship's party when we were both standing in the back of the room making remarks about the CO's wife. (That's what CO's wives are for—to help other people make friends.) Granted, Dawn is the only friend I ever met at one of these functions, but if I had not gone, I would never have met her. Just think, I could still be wearing white pantyhose with black skirts. All you've gotta do is say hello. A couple of hundred times.

You'll meet the powers that be. While you're at the party anyway, walk up to the spouses of the ombudsman, CO, XO, command master chief, or sergeant major and introduce yourself. You can tell who they are because they're usually older than you. Sometimes you don't have to find them; they'll walk right up and act friendly. But don't bet on it. Just as financial advisers tell you to meet the bank manager before you need a loan, experienced military spouses advise newcomers to meet the home guard before they've got a problem. Even if you think you won't ever need their help. You don't have to brownnose them or be their friend. This is a professional relationship; they understand that. Human beings sometimes swing things for people they know—but not for hostile strangers.

You'll get a night out with your guy. Hanging out with the people from work isn't the best of times for anybody. When you've done The Pretty for an hour or two, make your excuses and go do something fun. Which could mean you'll be bowling in an evening gown. You've already got the sitter. You're already out of the house. Now go have a good time. You two deserve it.

That is what Dear Abby and all those feminist folk are missing. A couple can bring things to the table that a husband or wife can't do on their own. It's a strength and a power. And the military knows it would be lost without it.

The Cast of Characters: Who Are These People and What Do They Want from Me?

Margaret Mead, the famous anthropologist, made her mark going into Samoa and reporting on how adolescents universally drive their mothers crazy, even without access to the Internet.

Me, I've spent my whole life studying native militarians. They are an interesting people, clad in colorful native dress and participating in bizarre social customs. They are evolving all the time. I like them.

I can see, however, how introducing yourself to the whole host of them at once could be a bit much. It's especially difficult for a person whose entire knowledge of the military is confined to the cast of *JAG, Top Gun,* and, possibly, *Black Hawk Down.*

The longer you live inside the military, the more you will notice every command has its own jolly little cast of characters. They're rigid. They're quirky. Not a one of them looks like Tom Cruise.

I know you're thinking I should arrange this section by order of rank, just like the military does. I should list everyone as officer or enlisted. I should describe everyone from the bottom up. I should spend a lot of time chatting about how to identify the woman Most Likely to Be Married to Someone Who Could Advance Your Husband's Career.

You have got to be kidding me.

How many times do I have to tell you? Other people's wives and their relationships with you (unless you cause them to commit a felony) have nothing to do with your husband's advancement. That poor guy is already busting his hump, learning his job, working sixteen or eighteen hours a day for some fruitloop who throws pens when he gets mad.

The service member knows more about how to cope with his career than you or I will ever know. Your sole job is to be the one true and loyal person in his life. The way he is the one true and loyal person in yours. It is hard enough to be home to each other without taking on responsibility for his career. You'll still worry about it, I know. I do it too. I worry about him getting promoted. I worry about him not getting promoted.

> **CHECKIST**   **What You Absolutely Have to Know about Your Spouse's Job**
>
> The first day your spouse comes home from his new command, sit the guy down with a frosty mug and write down the answers to these questions. Then tape them to the fridge. He should do the same on the first day of your new job.
>
> ✓ What is the exact name of your job?
>
> ✓ What does that mean? What will you do on the job?
>
> ✓ Who is your boss? What is the name of his job?
>
> ✓ Give me three phone numbers I can call in case of dire emergency. (Only one of these can be his cell phone number.)
>
> ✓ What is the name of your unit or department?
>
> ✓ How does your unit fit into the big picture? What is your mission?

I worry that people at work will think his favorite see-through undershirt is all my idea.

Often, when I find myself worrying about his career, it isn't because he isn't doing well enough. He's doing fine. I'm worried because *I'm* not doing well enough in my career, in my life. It's just easier to worry about his business than to do anything about my own.

Take an interest in the command's cast of characters strictly for your own sake. Think of the military as our own private Samoa. We can't get off the island until we figure the whole thing out.

Officer or Enlisted?

I read a story several years ago in the Letters to the Editor section of *Stars and Stripes,* the newspaper for American military posted overseas. In the letter, an enlisted man recounted how an admiral had asked a group of officers' wives to seat themselves in order of their rank. The women shuffled themselves around until they were in ranking order, right down to the number of days in grade. Just when they were reset-tled, the admiral blasted them. "You don't hold rank, ladies! Your hus-bands hold rank!" The snooty officers' wives were reduced to sobbing into their little pink handbags.

This story was told with much glee. But it never happened. It is an urban legend—like spider eggs in Bubble Yum, or the new sports car sold for one hundred dollars by a spiteful ex-wife. Every service offers its own version of the story.

The story illustrates the terrible animosity that once existed between the wives of enlisted men and those of officers. In the past, these rela-tionships were volatile for a reason—some wives were stuck up beyond belief and some wives were low class. It went both ways, I'm sure.

But the stereotype has really outlived its usefulness. Our experiences today are much more similar than they ever were in the past. That is a benefit to us all. Instead of an enlisted wives' club and an officers' wives' club, most commands now sponsor a unified Family Support Group or Family Readiness Group (with some additional social requirements, de-pending on how social your husband's job really is). If you attend enough of these events, you will run into both the snooties and the slobbies, I guarantee it. So that means we don't have to go, right?

Mentor, Mentor, Mentor

I got lucky. I met Char Foley, a Navy wife with more than thirty-three years married to the service. She took many young spouses under her wing. We were not her buddies;she had plenty of friends her own age. We simply ran into her at big functions or at the commis-sary a few times a year. She was always good for a little advice, a little encouragement, the answer to a question—she mentored us. Char didn't get a lot of mentoring or support as a young wife, but that only made her more determined to make life easier for other young spouses than it had been for her. Char found most military spouses don't need to be dragged along, they just need to talk to someone. "You can't pay people back," says Char, "but you can pass it on."

Wrong. Where did you get that idea? Not attending things only hurts you. It doesn't begin to cleaver the snooties or the slobbies. It only makes the normal people lonesome.

Here's a solution: Feel sorry for the "S" Brigade. Pity is a lovely thing. When you get cleavered by a snobby, feel sorry that she thinks her tenuous grasp on her husband's accomplishments entitles her to look down on others. Run into a slobby, and feel sorry that she has so many troubles on her plate that this is the best she can do. Keep a ten-year-long list of these poor creatures and you might fill it with a dozen people. What is that? Not enough to start an exercise class.

When I look at military spouses up and down the chain of command, I feel one thing: respect. I know the price each one of these people pays for building a life with a man or woman in uniform. I know what they suffer. I know their joys. Officer or enlisted? Who cares?

Junior Enlisted Spouses

Junior enlisted spouses get a bad rap. In *Invisible Women: Junior Enlisted Army Wives,* author Margaret C. Harrell identifies the typical stereotype we have for junior enlisted spouses as "lower class—and, thus, uneducated and unintelligent, out of control both sexually and reproductively, in unstable relationships and lacking morals, financially irresponsible, poorly groomed, inappropriately dressed, and lacking both proper manners and housekeeping skills."

That is an ugly stereotype. I'm sure you can trot out some poor little gal you knew long ago who fit every bit of that description and was mean as a bone to boot. But that doesn't mean most junior enlisted are like that. When you meet them and talk to them, you will find their biggest sin is that they are young. Painfully young. Sometimes they are just teenagers. They do what teenagers do. When military family building is difficult for women in their thirties and forties, is it any wonder that it's harrowing for these young women?

Harrell says that junior enlisted spouses often feel physically isolated, financially limited, dependent, and invisible. Whatever hits us hard hits them harder. While there is little we can do about their financial situations, their invisibility is our responsibility. You might not see enlisted junior spouses at your command functions, but you will see them in the commissary, at the pool, in Wal-Mart. They work at your dry cleaner, the exchange, the hospital, your own office. Look them in the eye and treat them as full-blooded members of the Homefront Club. They've earned it.

Senior Enlisted Spouses

The very moment they've had enough experience to be interesting, many wives of senior enlisted personnel drop off the face of the community. It's not really their fault. They've been burned so often by other military wives that a whole brigade of Shriners couldn't do anything to help.

But there is simply no replacement for their wisdom and experience.

They have been there and done that. A young spouse won't encounter anything that the senior spouse hasn't run up against before. Survivorship is everything.

They understand whining and complaining. These senior wives understand that all the whining and complaining they hear from younger wives is just that: whining and complaining. It doesn't mean anything. Good to hear it and let it go.

They look so tough. It is comforting to the young to know that marriages do survive military life; they do thrive under these conditions. That military marriage is, in fact, possible.

Senior enlisted spouses are an absolutely invaluable resource. What can we do to take better care of them? How can we let them know that we are not going to cleaver them?

Command Spouses

On October 12, 2000, the USS *Cole* pulled into the port of Aden, Yemen, for refueling. Suicide bombers blew a forty-by-forty-foot hole in the ship. The crew battled to keep her afloat. Seventeen sailors died.

That was a dark enough day for the Navy.

But when family members of the crew started to show up at a central meeting point awaiting word on their sailors, the Navy discovered there was neither a commanding officer's spouse nor an executive officer's spouse. No one was even nominally in charge. Although the ship had the required ombudsman, no formal spouses' group was in place. The people streaming through the door had never seen each other before that day. They had no camaraderie, no contact, no way to pass on information. And somehow, that made everything worse.

In recent years, command wives have won a measure of freedom from the stifling constrictions of times gone by. Command spouses are now told that they don't have to accept any role unless they want to. A flowchart is even available for those who fail to understand that the spouse's participation is simply not required.

Not required?

Who are they kidding? It is not okay to do nothing. The interested presence of the senior spouses, both officer and enlisted, is definitely required—if not by the military itself, then by our own humanity.

In recent years, many spouses have elected not to participate in a leadership role among the command's families. Some choose not to live in the area. Others decide that their lives are already too full to assume that much responsibility. Still others command ships of their own.

As a modern woman, I can understand that. I appreciate the hard-won privilege of participating or not, according to your own will. But no matter how valid the reason, rejecting the role that comes as part and parcel of your spouse's career sends a clear message to the entire command: Military families are not important. The Marine Corps is just a job. This is an Army of one. Deal with it.

Human compassion dictates that we reach out to ease the path of other travelers on the same journey. We are required to remember the experience of moving far from home, the pain of the first deployment, the struggle to make a fledgling marriage work. Being a command spouse doesn't mean massaging every person who comes across your path, fetching beer for every party, or ironing out everyone else's problems to the exclusion of your own. It does mean nurturing the idea that the military is not just a job but a community, a heritage, a way of life.

If you can't do it, follow the official guidelines and find a capable someone who wants to nurture those other families. If you are a commanding officer and you are unmarried, divorced, about-to-be-divorced, or a geographic bachelor, it is your duty to find an Alpha Female for the families of your unit and to recognize her as such. In return, the rest of us promise you Alpha Females that we'll try to stop being so critical. We will stop second-guessing the location of the Christmas party, the number of eggs at the Easter egg hunt, your proclivity for wearing leather pants, or whether your husband took the submarine out during the holidays just because he does not like you. We'll stop thinking you have any influence over promotions, hours on the job, duty nights, leave periods. We'll stop calling you at home, expecting you to do something about it.

We naturally give you power because of your position. Use it wisely and respectfully. We still expect you to find us a good ombudsman. We expect you to know where to find the answers to our questions. But we don't expect you to be Nancy Reagan, Julia Roberts, and Carmen Electra all wrapped into one. It's a two-way street. You agree to do the job, and we'll let you give it a whirl.

The USS *Cole* should be remembered for many reasons: the sacrifice of her crew, the pain of the nation, and the way the military family came together to take care of its own at home and abroad. The importance of having a responsible person take the role of command spouse is just one more to add to the list.

The Old Gals

At one time or another, you will meet the spouses of admirals and generals. This is unavoidable. Those highfliers are dying to talk to little you. So you supply your name. You get into a short conversation and say

Ombudsmen and Key Spouses: What Do They Do and Should You Be One?

The most carefully spelled-out roles in the military are those of ombudsman and Marine Corps key spouse. These sainted individuals go through a huge amount of training on how to help troubled members of the command. It's a wonder they can remember all of that information and still tie their shoes.

These are unpaid positions and they aren't for everyone, especially anyone who is simply trying to advance her spouse's career. What they do offer is a meaningful place to volunteer and contribute.

Take on this job only if you feel the calling and have the biggest heart; the most logical, well-organized mind; and the innate ability to keep your mouth absolutely shut. When your command is blessed with a wonderful ombudsman, treasure her. Drop a flower on her doorstep. Or a note. Or a coconut cake. I always think a coconut cake is just the thing to express real appreciation.

something idiotic. Or something that seemed okay at the time, but seems catastrophically idiotic when you are wide awake that night. Resist the urge to pop up and call the general's wife to apologize or, worse, explain what you meant. She met a hundred people that day. She doesn't remember your faux pas. She doesn't have the energy to pick apart conversations. Senior wives are just glad that someone friendly bothered to speak to them. They remember what it was like to be you. Don't sweat the small stuff.

Women in the Service

When I was in school, I wandered into the Air Force recruiter's office one rainy afternoon. I think I was lost. But the guy was all over me in an instant. Loved the idea of my pilot father and ROTC brother. Loved my major. Loved my 20/13 vision.

"You could be a pilot!" he crowed.

One small problem: I took great pride in the fact that I had not run since puberty. Not one step. I knew all about the opportunities the military had to offer. I also knew there was no way I was (or ever would be) tough enough to lace up the combat boots and go get it.

But Lord, I admire the women who do. I root for them.

One of the blessings my marriage has brought me is a position firmly on the Girl Team. I never say women don't understand me (anymore). I'm never (well, hardly ever) trying to be the cutest thing in the room. Men are darling creatures, but they have a team of their own.

So nothing annoys me more than when women criticize other women on the team—especially those in uniform. I can't stand to hear women parrot on about how the military made a "suicidal" mistake when it allowed women in combat and threw away the "mystique" of an all male force. Or that the military has been dumbed down to accommodate women. Or how all the women in uniform are "trying" to get pregnant before deployment.

I hear that load of malarkey and want to snap somebody's bra strap. Some women in uniform are dirtbags—probably in the same proportion that some men in uniform are dirtbags. Men have their own ways of getting into trouble and missing deployment. I wish we were all 100 percent behind our women in the service. But our confusion spans the country. On the one hand, we have a congressionally mandated dual-sex military. On the other hand, during the war in Iraq, senior officers wondered what kind of country sends one-hundred-pound young women to fight their battles for them.

That isn't my worry. I am not shocked to see women—mommies, even—in combat. Women in uniform must mean women in combat. Married or unmarried, with or without children. Combat is part of the job.

We know that. The young women who join the military today understand that too. They aren't complaining. They need the money, the on-the-job training, the benefits, the possibilities. No one tricks them into it. Like their male counterparts, something in them cries out to leave the place where they were brought up. Watching your friends take jobs at Wal-Mart or Exxon mini-marts must cause a soul-deep longing to go somewhere else, to do something different.

Joining the military is a good, strong way to get out of a small town or a small world without money and without education. It takes courage to leave what you know. That alone deserves our respect and our support.

What about Single Mothers in Combat?

While most of us will accept the idea of a woman in uniform who does everything (or more) that a man does, I think we need to look more closely at our attitudes toward mothers in combat. This may be where a slice of our national character is revealed, because the military is no easy job for a single mother.

While there may be a slacker or two out there in uniform, the military is not glorified welfare. It requires a long workweek, overnight duty, complicated child care. It requires you to beg your parents, your sister, your friend to take care of your child for six or eight or ten months at a time. It's chock-full of the kind of sexual harassment that makes the papers. There are always people insinuating that you got your position based on gender, not merit.

Being in the military is so hard that single mothers in uniform often start informal support groups within their commands. They help each other out with child care when their normal providers bail. They talk and sympathize. They expect one another to be good mothers, good soldiers, good sailors. They give each other hell when they don't live up to the standard.

When we civilians talk about women in uniform, we act as though these single mothers are heartless and don't understand how painful a separation might be to a child. Could anything be further from the truth? Maybe we ought to spend our energy examining why single moms are willing to risk deployment and war to stay in the military.

Could it be that they have looked at all their options and this is the best chance they have to make a life for themselves and their children? They know that separations are hard on their children. Separations are hard on them too. They are the ones who come home from deployment to find that their toddler rushes right past them with a skinned knee to get to Grandma.

That draws heart's blood from a mother. You probably couldn't stand it. I know I couldn't. It's a good thing I don't have to.

To a high school graduate with kids, though, the military means a secure and steady paycheck. It means benefits. It means that her kids can see a dentist even if their father never comes through with the child-support check. It means when the kids get an ear infection, they get the pink stuff. It means she has made her children safe.

I don't think we should be ashamed that our country sends women into battle. They do us proud. Instead, maybe we should be ashamed that in a country as rich as ours, these women weigh their options, factor in their children's pain, and still decide that the military is their safest bet. Despite the long separations and the risk of war or capture or even death.

We should be ashamed that this is their best option. We don't need a law to keeps mothers out of combat. We need a national spirit that works to offer small-town girls and inner-city girls many more options.

We on the Girl Team, especially those of us who are married to the military, ought to be the first ones to offer them a hand.

Never Stop Learning

They keep telling us that the more we get to know about the military, the easier it will be to navigate our way around. Yeah, yeah, yeah. We know we should, but it's one more thing to add to the to-do list.

Luckily for us, the military is making this easier all the time. You can buy one of the many guidebooks for military spouses that tell you how to read a Leave and Earnings Statement, how to get your dental benefits, and where to find phone numbers for every military organization in the country. Or you can stop by your Family Support Center to find out about the classes they offer, pick up their brochures, take a tour of the base. This is all great stuff.

When it comes to family team building, though, the Marine Corps has taken the lead with its Lifestyle Insights, Networking, Knowledge and Skills (LINKS) Program. Instead of expecting you to read up on all this baffling info, the program offers a daylong event—sort of a Military Wife 101 class, taught by trained mentors. The Navy has followed suit with a program called Compass.

Nice. Helpful for others. But do we really hafta go? Sure you do. You might find that every minute of the day is relevant to you or you might pick up just one nugget about the baffling nature of Tricare. You might even find someone who knows a good babysitter. The powers that be want you to have this knowledge. It's a pain. But if you learn even one thing, you could save yourself more than a day of heartache. What is that worth?

3 A Life of Your Own

Finding, Getting, and Doing the Work You Love

I KNOW I AM NOT everything my husband needs in his life. I don't even come close. I am his Only Love, his best friend, his confidante. The mother of his children. His Go-to Gal. I am the only person on earth who understands (and caters to) his complicated arrangement of bed pillows.

I am his wife. But I am not his everything. And he is not mine.

I don't mean that in a women's magazine sort of way. I don't mean that idea that married people are attached like Post-It Notes—easy to stick together, joined for a convenient period, peeling apart without ever leaving a mark.

In our military marriage, our bones are knit together. Our fates entwined. Our DNA blended in three little people who think we ought to stay together even though I cannot be trusted to operate the printer.

But we can't possibly rely on each other to fulfill our every need. It isn't realistic; it isn't fair. We both need meaningful work. We both need to tend to parents, siblings, friends, and tastes of our own from time to time. My husband is interested in *Smithsonian* magazine, drill bits, and basketball games that always end exactly the same way—a soap opera for guys. I like lovely fabric stores and lively book clubs and seeing movies in an actual darkened theater. With popcorn, not Goobers.

Criminy, what kind of person goes to a theater wanting *Goobers?*

I understand what the experts mean when they say the best marriages include a little separation, a little time to miss each other. I recognize that some of our divorcing friends don't actually need a divorce as much as they need a long, long break from each other. I can see that a little time off from the stress and strain of marriage, to take a class or complete a work project, could be very helpful.

So why do I dread this kind of separation, this kind of break, this kind of freedom every time it comes up—especially when it comes compliments of the United States military?

Perhaps because it comes in fits and starts. Instead of three or four years to concentrate on finishing school or establishing a career, we get six months here, a year there, twenty minutes someplace else. That is not the usual way to establish yourself as a serious professional. Everyone knows that, particularly military wives.

We are an orderly lot. We like to be able to plan ahead. It feels like these dribbles of time aren't enough to do anything, especially anything having to do with a career. It feels like you'll spend twenty of your most productive, moneymaking years following that Man in Uniform from base to tiny base, town to tiny town. What can one little woman possibly do with that?

You'll be surprised.

When Will You Stop Blaming Him?

I remember exactly when my military life took a turn for the much, much better. I had just finished my monthly I'm-never-going-to-be-anything-have-anything-or-do-anything-as-long-as-you-are-in-the-stupid-military fit. I had these a lot. It wasn't pretty. But it felt so normal at the time.

So, after slamming the bedroom door until the foundation shuddered, I stormed down the stairs. I can still see them. The red carpet runner needed vacuuming. Dust motes drifted down in a sunbeam. The dent and scrape on the overhang still stood out from where the movers tried to shove the queen-size box spring up the narrow steps.

Then, a voice in my head clearly asked, *"When are you going to stop blaming him?"*

I stopped right there on the steps, under that ugly mattress scrape. Because at that very moment, I had to face the fact that I *had* been blaming him. For everything. For a very long time.

For the previous nine years, I had been blaming my husband and his job for all the ambitions I had folded up and put away. I knew my problem wasn't him. It wasn't that we had a couple of kids or that we had moved eight times in nine years. My problem was me.

I was experiencing the same kind of frustration that every stay-at-home mom experiences from time to time. You love those kids. You know you're doing right by them. But you have the sensation that you're trapped by baby gates and safety caps. You're treading water in a sea of juice boxes and Matchbox cars. Your brain is leaking out of your ears from endless renditions of "Goodnight comb/And goodnight brush/ Goodnight nobody/Goodnight mush." Being prodded by the demands of the military doesn't make it any easier.

At that moment on the stairs, I had to acknowledge that it wasn't Brad or Brad's job holding me back. It was me. It was me insisting on being a civilian. It was me wanting to have the same kind of life everyone else had—or what I thought they had. It was so much easier to blame him and his job than it was to figure out what I had to do so I could become the person I wanted to be.

Could I really stop just because I told myself to stop? The military was my favorite target. So big, so powerful, so unaware of me. It wasn't going to be easy to give up blaming Brad.

Every woman I know who has a life of her own and a military husband once had that moment of ultra-self-awareness. After she spewed her allotted share of blame, she decided to pick herself up and do something else.

What Else Can She Do?

What else can a woman do when she knows she has to take responsibility for her own ambitions? Almost anything.

The day I walked down the steps and stopped blaming the Navy was the same day I finally wrote to the editor of our city paper, explaining why he needed a military spouse columnist—and why it should be me.

What does a woman do when she stops blaming the military for her career problems? She starts trolling the career section of the bookstore. She browses course catalogues from adult education programs, community colleges, chef schools, and the local four-year university. She asks the Family Service Center where she can get help with her job hunt. New programs open all the time. Women who stop blaming the military do what it takes—even if they are poor or uneducated or very young.

Take this story, for example.

A girl from a little town called Niceville, located near a big military base, fell in love with a boy in the grocery store where she worked as a cashier. They married a month after her high school graduation. He enlisted in the military. She got pregnant. They moved to his first assignment.

So what do you think happened next?

If you've lived near a military base long enough, I bet you're guessing that the girl from Niceville dissolved into tears every time the word d-e-p-l-o-y-m-e-n-t was mentioned. Or that she ran up $12,000 worth of credit card debt at Baby Gap. Or she ate so many Krispy Kremes that she was literally sitting around her house.

Guess again.

In this story, Kristina Clancy, twenty years old, knew she had to find work and probably go back to school. But the thought of taking on debt for education, when she and her husband never had any debt before, was daunting.

Certain that there had to be a program, grant, or scholarship to help military spouses find jobs, Kristina got out her phone book and started calling all of the local places. Navy Fleet and Family Service Center, Kee Business College, Sentera School of Health, Tidewater Tech. None of them knew of any program that could help her. Even her husband, John, finally concluded they'd have to do it themselves.

"I know there's something out there," Kristina told him, thinking that with their tight budget, even ten dollars would help. "And I'm going to find it."

Right. The rest of us oh-so-experienced military types would probably have agreed with Kristina's husband. Aren't military spouses considered just a form of cheap labor that keeps the economy running on low gear? Wouldn't we assume that the only thing a girl like Kristina could expect is some silly program about building a resume or leads on minimum-wage slavery at call centers? We would be wrong.

A New Directive

The decision to stay in the Navy is not made around the wardroom table. It is made around the kitchen table.
—Rear Admiral Jay Foley, USN (Ret.)

In recent years, the military has become more aware of the importance of finding good work for military spouses. A spouse's employment or unemployment obviously affects the family's standard of living and child-care arrangements. The military also has discovered that the spouse's employment situation affects recruitment, relocation, and, most importantly, retention.

In the *1999 Active Duty Member Survey,* service members whose spouses were employed or voluntarily out of the workforce were found to be more satisfied with military life than were other members. In fact, the Army Personnel Survey Office announced that the number one reason a soldier stays in the Army is that his spouse supports his career.

That's right, wife units. We are the military's Number One Retention Tool. Which we knew all along. Please send my bonus directly to my home. Encased in a BMW Z3, thanks. Red, definitely red.

Anyway, ever since they discovered how darn important our work actually is to our husbands, more funds and programs have been directed toward finding employment for employment-seeking military spouses.

Kristina Clancy found a program called NEXStep Training for Transition. Funded by a $20 million grant from the U.S. Department of Labor, it provides free career counseling and training for military spouses. Kristina went to the NEXStep office three times. Her caseworker asked her to answer some questions and to take a couple of tests. Kristina was required to research her area of interest—she wanted to become an LPN or a medical assistant. She followed up often to make sure she had done everything possible for her case to be approved by the board. It was.

The girl from Niceville attended night classes at Tidewater Tech to become a medical assistant while her husband parented their six-month-old daughter, Kalaya. And NEXStep paid her tuition. Kristina had to talk to her case manager monthly and show her report card to keep the money coming.

The woman who stops blaming lets herself dream other dreams. She makes herself do scary things—like interviewing, networking, applying, studying, and calling and calling and calling.

I spent the first nine years of my marriage clearly defining the ten thousand ways the military wasn't fair to spouses. Shoot, I could have spent twenty years bashing my head against that brick wall.

You can do that too. Or you can be like Kristina and lift your head away to see the width, depth, and breadth of that wall. Like her, you can go over it, under it, through it, or around it. Don't waste nine years. Don't waste two. Resolve to stop blaming the military for the speed bump it set in your career path. Start now.

Composing a Life

"What do you do?"

It's an innocuous question, but one that many military spouses dread. In this era of burgeoning opportunities for women, we feel almost guilty admitting that we haven't just come back from orbiting the earth or collecting our Nobel Peace Prize.

How liberated does it sound to admit you spent your week nursing everyone in the family through the flu, fixing a roast for dinner, driving six preschoolers to a concert, and mailing thousands of invitations on time? How successful does it sound to confess you finally found a job that fits with your military family life and pays all the school fees—but has nothing to do with those four, five, six years you spent in college?

In her book *Composing a Life,* anthropologist Mary Catherine Bateson writes that when it comes to defining a successful life, American women have "over-focused on the stubborn struggle toward a single goal . . . We see achievement as purposeful and monolithic . . . rather than something crafted from odds and ends."

In other words, it is easy to admire a person who has pursued one career goal—from point A to point Z. It's easy to admire a service member who has a resume written in gold braid across his chest. It's easy to admire a man in uniform.

It is harder to admire the woman next to him who must create a life from whatever is on hand. Her life rarely, if ever, runs according to plan. She may start with a career every bit as grand as his. However, unless she and her husband plan to spend a lot of time living apart, her career is easily blown off course—no matter what the recruiters say.

The accomplishments of a military spouse are never laid out in an easy-to-read, straight line. Instead, she has multiple commitments to her husband, her children, her hobbies, her work, her home, her education, her parents, her church. Instead of a straight line, Bateson points out, this kind of life is a pattern, a creative work put together in stages.

That can be a very good thing. It's hard to see when you're living the disappointments and detours, but a delight to look back upon in later years.

Older friends have told me that women sometimes make the mistake of looking back and assessing their lives when they turn forty—the same time in life that men tend to take stock. Instead, my friends say, we should plan to judge our lives at fifty—an age when the years of child

Message to Stay-at-Home Mothers

Many military spouses opt to be a stay-at-home mother when their children are small. If that's you, you're probably working harder than you ever thought possible, right there at home. Please, don't skip the following pages, assuming they're not aimed at you. Remember, five or six years down the road, you will be freer to pursue other aspects of your life. Even the prospect of a long-deferred dream can help in the here and now.

rearing and the demands of the military usually are ending. Don't be afraid that everyone else is getting ahead of you. You've got more time than you think.

Bad News First: The Five Enemies of Your Career Ambitions

What is the economy up to? We have no idea. Sometimes when the economy is down, military wives are hit pretty hard. Seems like there is nothing left at the buffet when we come to town. Other times, the economy affects us not at all. The rest of the world might be unemployed, but we slide right into a fabulous made-for-me kind of job. Military spouses have to survey the landscape wherever we live and then do what we have to do. We make our own luck.

Before we get into strategies to power through the Ambition Speed Bump, let's take a real good look at the speed bump itself. Here are the most common complaints I hear about combining military marriage and career.

Enemy #1: Frequent Moves and Absences

No sooner do you make a plan and start working on it than your husband comes home with PCS orders to Never-heard-of-it, USA—for four years. That's too long to send him off alone, too long to collect unemployment. Even if you do find work you like, your husband's frequent absences will make coleslaw out of your child-care situation.

Enemy #2: Jobs That Don't Travel

Theorem: *The more specific your career, the more difficult it is to find employment in another town.* Even if you are the world's foremost surfboard waxer, you won't find much of a market for your product three states away from the nearest ocean.

Theorem: *The more successful you are in one location, the more unlikely it is that you will find a job at the same level at a new duty station.* If you're the anchorwoman at a Boston television station, you might be able to find work at a television station in Hawaii. But, even in a smaller market, they will probably prefer the anchorwoman they already have.

Enemy #3: Military Bases in Small Markets

When you're yearning for a career, you're blessed if you're sent to a nice big town like Chicago or Washington, D.C. Jobs abound. Sometimes, though, you are sent to towns too small to have their own Taco Bell. If it's a particularly small place, the available jobs may be far away, pay minimum wage, and not be worth the cost of the drive. A depressed economy means even less opportunity for military spouses.

Enemy #4: Job Saturation

You may train for a job in a profession that moves easily, like nursing or teaching, then move to a new duty station and find the hospitals and schools are already full of military spouses who trained for jobs that move easily, like nursing or teaching. Arrggh!

Enemy #5: Perception

The obstacles that often frustrate us the most are negative perceptions, prejudices, and stereotypes. Some employers believe military spouses are unreliable, likely to move, and likely to bail during deployment. According to the U.S. Department of Labor, we're just as likely to stay at a job as long as most civilians. Unfortunately, the label "military spouse" can still be a strike against us.

How Do You Get around All That?

You can go to Amazon.com and find a gazillion books about how to get a job. You can read 'em all, but they won't help you combine a military marriage with your own soaring (or modest) ambitions. What you need to do is apply one of the secrets of the Homefront Club.

We club members know that when it comes to getting over those career speed bumps, you've got exactly two choices:

1. Choose a portable career, independent of geography.

2. Go to work *expecting* glitches to pop up.

Some secret. Two measly choices—neither of which is appealing in any way, shape, or form. You have to remember that once you marry into the military, you are no longer following some small, narrow, pre-set career path for one little person. You and your husband are *composing a life*. A big, complex life. We're talking about a huge, woman-sized, multidimensional, international kind of life here.

Here's another secret: Remember to keep your eyes on the prize. That would be you at fifty years old, still married to your spiffy man-who-must-be-in-uniform, surrounded by your family, dogs, friends, house, white couch—and a lifetime of meaningful, rewarding work.

Flexibility Pays Off with Portable Job

Marine Corps spouse Terry Gruny has moved four times during the past eight years. She's worked from home for Innovative Graphic Systems, Inc. (IGS), the whole time. Terry began working for IGS when she was posted to Monterey, California, and she's carried her job with her from Washington, D.C., to Camp LeJeune, and back to D.C.

At first, she just kept her boss's calendar and checked his spelling. Now, she's the contract manager, payroll administrator, bookkeeper, secretary to the president, and Web administrator. How did she convince her boss to let her take her job with her? She was flexible and made herself indispensable.

"I think that if you work from home, you better be flexible," says Terry. For her, that means postponing dinner and talking to her boss for an hour every night by cell phone as he commutes home. It means answering the phone on the weekends and sometimes on vacation.

"In return, I get as much vacation and time off as I desire," says Terry. When her husband deployed during Operation Iraqi Freedom, her boss, Bill, was especially understanding. "During the four months of the war, Bill only asked me to keep track of the money, and the rest could wait. I'm on my fourth move, and I know he'll wait patiently for at least thirty days before he expects me to be up and running. How much do I appreciate my boss? Words cannot express."

Geography-free jobs don't typically start out that way. Usually, military wives start with a regular, tied-to-the-desk job. After they've proven themselves and built a reputation, employers are more willing to consider letting them carry their jobs to a new city and telecommute. This works well especially in large corporations with more than one location.

Worthwhile Web Sites for Spouses

The Military Spouse Career Network at www.mscn.org is a great supplement to the Family Member Employment Assistance Program and the Spouse Employment Assistance Program on your base. The site offers career information to military spouses, including information on telecommuting, unemployment compensation, employment with the federal government, and continuing education.

The site also includes a variety of articles on all aspects of employment, such as pursuing college while your partner is on active duty. It's worth every minute of your time. Also try the U.S. Department of Labor's web site, www.milspouse.org, which provides information about employment and training opportunities for military spouses.

Shifting Gears

Often, we land in a new community and find there are just no opportunities for our big career as a stevedore, a snowmobile repairman, or an entomologist studying the mating behavior of the glassy-winged sharpshooter in the Napa Valley vineyards.

Sometimes, the best way to find satisfying employment is to get off the track we've been on, to shift gears. What else would you like to do? Get a new job? Stay home with the kids? Go back to school? All of the above?

Robbie Piel, twenty-nine, and his wife, Sheri, twenty-eight, met when he was a high school sophomore in Garland, Texas. "Right after high school, I knew I wanted to marry her," said Piel. "I needed some way to support us while she went all the way through college and med school."

Piel trained as an emergency medical technician and paramedic in Dallas. In addition to teaching and studying martial arts on weekends (he currently holds nine black belts in seven different martial arts), Piel considered becoming a weekend warrior in the reserves.

The Navy did not have a program that suited him. But the recruiter was very interested in Sheri—especially when he heard about her medical school test scores.

"He told me all about the program. I had to run back to the station to call my wife and tell her all about it. She was skeptical, of course, but I got her to talk to a recruiter."

When Sheri joined the Navy just before medical school, Piel knew he would eventually have to move. Hours of watching Food TV at the fire station while waiting for the next emergency confirmed that he would like to work in the culinary arts.

"I've always loved to cook," said Piel. "My grandmother says I was in the kitchen trying to help her out as soon as I could walk."

Robbie and Sheri looked into duty stations where she could work and he could go to culinary school. Norfolk had everything.

"When it really came time that we were definitely going to have to move and I was going to either have to transfer my paramedic certification to another state or choose another career field, I decided I wasn't happy being a paramedic anymore. I chose to drop that altogether."

Although it is common for military wives to follow their spouses from duty station to duty station, things seem to work differently for many men—especially when it comes to changing their role as primary breadwinner.

"It was a little unnerving to leave my position because I was making exceptional money when I left," confessed Piel. "But I

Why Can't He Be a Geographic Bachelor?

Sometimes it seems like the best way to keep your career is to encourage your spouse to toddle off to his next duty station alone. After all, he's only going to deploy half the time you're there, right?

Don't even think about it. Doing a tour as a geographic bachelor is a major step, far more expensive than you could ever imagine and far more stressful than any couple will admit.

Ask yourself these questions before you condemn yourself and your spouse to the Styrofoam lifestyle:

1. Is it for longer than one year?
2. Will the separation burden the marriage as much as an extra deployment or a back-to-back deployment?
3. Have you been married less than ten years?
4. Is he such a difficult person that it's easier to live apart from him than to live with him?
5. Is it worth it?

A teacher might need to stay until the end of the school year. A mom with kids in school might need to stay with them to finish a semester while her husband moves ahead to his next job. A senior in high school should not be moved. But never, never choose to be apart just to make more money. It is never worth it. Ask around.

don't have any problem with her making the money. I'm all for it. It's worked out really well so far."

Everything seems to be working out well. Piel enrolled in Johnson and Wales University and made the dean's list every semester. He was inducted into the Silver Key Honor Society. Although he was accepted for a co-op position at the prestigious Inn at Little Washington in Washington, Virginia, he accepted an offer in Grand Summit, Utah, instead. It would be better for his career, because his interests run primarily toward fine southwestern cuisine.

"I'm looking forward to everything but the forty-five-hour drive," says Piel. And the separation from his wife. But he and Sheri have had to cope with that during her training.

"You basically have to make the best of it," says Piel. "You carry on your day-to-day life. I know we're faithful to each other. Probably because we've been together so long and have done so much growing together that we know each other better than anyone."

What Else Is There?

Sometimes getting a job just isn't kickin' it. The right thing simply isn't available. You won't be stationed in the area more than a few months. It isn't the right time of life to pursue a particular position. Or the jobs you're offered make you so depressed that you crawl into a bath of Hershey's syrup every night. So what else do you do if you're a full-fledged (albeit unwilling) member of the Homefront Club?

Starbucking

> *star-buck-ing*, v.: taking a job for which you are vastly overqualified, in a place that you enjoy, just to have something to do.

I go to my local Starbucks to work at least three times a week. I am not actually employed by the Starbucks corporation. I'm more about renting office space from them for the cost of a Grande-Skim-Two-Equal Latte. And a brownie.

But I may just work for Starbucks as a barista someday. It's a job I'd like—people, coffee, a place to go everyday where someone would notice if I did not show up. It isn't exactly in my field, but it would give form and structure to my day—something I need quite a lot of. Something we all need at one time or another.

If you find yourself at a duty station (particularly if you'll be living there less than a year) that does not offer much by way of career opportunities, try a few months of starbucking. After all, the vacuum tracks can only be so fresh. You can't make Thanksgiving dinner every day.

Find a little job. Maybe your version of Starbucks is a restaurant with a good atmosphere. Maybe a favorite store at the mall, a makeup counter, an art supply store. It might be an expensive furniture spot that offers employee discounts, or even a video arcade. Shop around before you apply. Starbucking is meant to be enjoyable—especially if it isn't high paying or career enhancing.

Stay open to the pleasure of it, to the variety of people you might meet. Lucky people make their own luck. You'd be very surprised where starbucking might lead.

Self-Employment

For most civilians, self-employment presents the big bugaboo—*no benefits*. No medical, no dental, no retirement, no security. No nothin'. Married to the military, this is not your problem. You still have to save for retirement. You still have to pay your own income tax and social security. But your medical and dental are covered. Heck, you can be a freelance columnist if you want. How impractical is that?

Not as impractical as you might think. Setting your own schedule, working without making child-care arrangements, and living in your flannel jammies with the snowmen on them can be very practical indeed. But it's tricky.

You can't do just anything and expect it to sell. You have to offer a service or product that people actually need, at a price they can afford. You have to make your skills, your ideas, and your talents dovetail with the marketplace.

That's what makes home sales, like Tupperware, Discovery Toys, Longaberger Baskets, Mary Kay, and Avon, so attractive to military spouses. The work appears to fit our lives. Surely you can sell that stuff anywhere. The problem is, home-based sales depend on your knowing lots of other people who know lots of other people with plenty of disposable income and unlimited time to attend sales parties.

How many people do you know who fit this description? How often have you really been glad to get an invitation to a home sales "party"? Lots of your potential friends don't think of these events as parties. They are pressure. And, thus, it clashes directly with the military spouse value of treasuring our friends. Real friends don't send their friends invitations to sales parties—they meet you for lunch instead.

Fewer than 10 percent of military wives are self-employed, according to *Jobs and the Military Spouse: Married, Mobile, and Motivated for the New Job Market,* by Janet I. Farley. It isn't an easy gig. But some military spouses do manage.

Lori McElroy, a military spouse of thirteen years, woke up one day and found that her husband had orders to Tunisia. As in *Africa.* They don't have Starbucks in Tunisia. They don't even have a Target. If you aren't working eight to five in the American embassy compound, you aren't working. Since Lori's boys were both in school, she had time on her hands.

What to do? When she was in her twenties, Lori had worked selling cards for Hallmark before she married Ken. She loved beautiful papers and creative stamping. *But they didn't have anything like that over there.* Cha-ching.

A Season for Everything

You might notice a difference in the wife requirements during different tours. When your husband is at sea or at an operational command, you may get a barrage of invitations to support groups, command parties, Hails, Farewells, luncheons. On shore, especially in Washington, D.C., or at certain training commands, the requirements for spouses are at a minimum. For most people, it's a down time, which is a good thing. A season of minimal involvement in the military, followed by a season of moderate or maximum involvement, is good for the marriage. Take advantage of a shore/training command to spend more time as a family and to invest in yourself.

So Lori started her own card business in Tunisia. Americans and Europeans needed her product—her cards were lovely, innovative, affordable. She liked making them. She found her supplies on the Internet and through catalogues. Mostly, though, she picked them up on buying trips to the United States and Europe. Would this idea work just anywhere? Probably not. It's easier for people to pick up a birthday card at Kroger than to buy ahead from a supplier like Lori. But Lori took advantage of her unique military situation and personal talents.

Keep your head up. If you are self-motivated enough to read a book, you are bright enough to find something that suits you.

Community Activism (aka Volunteering)

One of my neighbors used to say that her time was valuable. "I don't believe in volunteering," she said. "If people want me to work, they better be prepared to pay for my time."

I could understand why she felt that way. It's good to value yourself. But Homefront Clubbers report that volunteerism is often used as a trial period. Certain organizations always seem to hire from within—the devil-you-know, so to speak. They like to know if a person is dependable, friendly, smart, kind. Volunteering is a great way to make yourself an insider in a short time. Good volunteers often become employees—especially in schools.

Sometimes, volunteering in a job for which you would ordinarily be paid feels beneath you. Instead, think of it as training. Don't volunteer for every single thing that comes down the pike. Concentrate your community activism in one or two fields—desktop publishing, politics, retail, accounting. Whatever. For example, if you want to be a caterer or party planner, always volunteer for balls or command parties—jobs that require getting people, food, and music in the same place at the same time. Keep a notebook to remind yourself how all of your small efforts are adding up to a big accomplishment.

Full-Time Parenting

Guess what? As job loving as we military spouses can be, we can't be job loving all the time. Many military spouses (even those who were former

Volunteer for the Command?

Volunteer for the command only if it is your natural calling. Don't do it thinking you are helping your husband's career. You can't. Remember, military spousehood is another one of those pass/fail exercises. Just showing up to support your own spouse is plenty.

However, if you feel a call to volunteer inside the command—or if your spouse is the commanding officer, executive officer, command master chief, or master sergeant—it may be a good place to volunteer. They really need you. They need you more than the fourth-grade room mother, the Cub Scout pack, and the SPCA combined.

If you don't fit well in your current command (everybody feels this way once in a while), you may be better off volunteering with another group. Try a base-wide wives group, thrift store, mom's group, local school, or the Red Cross. Larger organizations tend to be a little less critical, a little less rankist, while still giving you a chance to get involved in the community and meet other people.

enlisted or officers themselves) find there comes a time when they need to do a season as a full-time parent. Blue's Clues 24/7. Bob the Builder all the time. Battlefield conditions like G. I. Joe would not believe.

Full-time parenting can be very good for military children. Even if the family is moving frequently or the father is absent, having one parent consistently at home can give children a feeling of stability—and it cuts down on child-care costs at the same time.

A recent Department of Defense study found that 37 percent of enlisted wives and 48 percent of officers' wives were neither employed nor seeking employment. The study did not say how many of these wives were full-time mothers, but I'm guessing that most of them were. How do they manage to do that?

But is full-time parenting for you? Deciding to be a full-time, stay-at-home parent is major. One of the best sources of information I've found on the subject is the National Association of At-Home Mothers (www.athomemothers.com). For one dollar per article, you can download information on topics including financial issues, benefits to your kids, discussions to have with your spouse, and how to keep your professional skills up to date.

Remember, staying home with your kids *is* a career choice.

Don't make it harder than it has to be. Don't think that you have to be ultra-mom in every aspect of your life to justify your presence at home. You don't have to be a full-time volunteer. You don't have to homeschool. You don't have to teach your children to play violin. Being a full-time parent is job enough for anyone.

Learning to be at home takes time. This isn't an easy profession. It takes management and leadership and rock-solid self-esteem. I've been working at it for fourteen years. At first, I could not imagine what full-time moms found to do with their time. *Ha!* As a stay-at-home parent, I could fill a thirty-six-hour day, easy.

Meet other moms. Your best support as a stay-at-home mom is other stay-at-home moms. In the baby and toddler years, these chicks are hard to meet because they are *at home.* Troll for other moms at the park, Gymboree, command parties, church nurseries, preschool parking lots. Get to it. Your best friend is waiting for you.

Hobbies

If getting a job just isn't practical, you're not up for volunteering, or you have your hands full with the kids, this could be the right time to pursue a hobby. Unlike the rest of your life, a hobby is something that stays finished. A hobby is something that you actually want to do. A hobby brings you into the sphere of other like-minded people.

Look for classes on scrapbooking, quilting, cross-stitching, and other handwork. Some towns have whole shops devoted to these hobbies. Adult sport leagues for soccer, ice hockey, figure skating, basketball, and volleyball are gaining momentum all over the country. Participating in martial arts, like karate and tae kwon do, can give you a real sense of accomplishment and measurable progress that you can bring with you from one duty station to the next. Is there anything more impressive than being a third-degree black belt? Hot diggity dog. They'll make you Homefront Queen with that kind of accomplishment.

I have found that Weight Watchers is an ideal spot to meet other military wives. Just like the rest of the country, we military spouses struggle with the scale. Weight Watchers offers a positive meeting every week, as well as an opportunity to get to know other members. Exercise classes and weight rooms—especially the ones devoted solely to women—lift the body and the spirit.

If you're strapped for cash, don't worry; many hobbies are inexpensive or virtually free. Walking, running, biking, and training for a marathon are affordable options. Keep up with the world via e-mail. Write

What about Church, Synagogue, or Mosque?

Don't forget religious services. Even if nothing could take the place of your church, synagogue, or mosque back home. Even if you weren't terribly devout in your teens and twenties. Even if you don't feel like getting up to go. Getting back to the faith can be an important step in your adulthood—particularly your military adulthood.

One of my readers reminded me recently that the old saw about how God doesn't give you more than you can handle isn't quite true. "It's not true that God gives us only what we can handle; sometimes he gives us more than we can bear so that we will turn to Him for help." God can be the best support when we are challenged by military life.

Becoming an attending member of a congregation offers God a way to get into our lives. Attend every week, even if it feels like you aren't getting much out of it. It is your faithfulness that matters. Often, I will enter the pew and realize that the only praying I've done that week is a scrambled "Bless Us Oh Lord . . ." over the spaghetti sauce. No wonder the week didn't go that well.

One of the best ways to feel at home in a new community is to volunteer in church. My own mother joined the church choir within a month of every move. Volunteering as a lector or in the church nursery not only helps you meet people, it also makes you visible in the church community. That way, when you attend the potlucks and the summer picnics, you'll know the other members. That can't happen if you just come on Sundays and sit in the pew.

letters to your grandma. Trace your ancestry. Play Bunko with the neighbors. Attend financial-aid classes or adult education classes held at local high schools. Check out a Family Readiness Group meeting.

Surprisingly, hobbies often turn into jobs. You get your black belt and they ask you to teach. You meet someone in your scrapbooking class who is looking for an employee with typing skills. Quilters get jobs at fabric stores. Weight Watchers looks for receptionists. Figure skaters get asked to teach creative movement. It doesn't happen the first day. But it does happen.

A Life Composed— One Duty Station at a Time

All of these suggestions sound good. But has anyone ever really managed to make them work? Of course.

Carrie Goodman leads a life so appealing, she belongs in a Nicholas Sparks novel. Friends come to lunch served on Blue Willow china in rooms decorated in blues and whites, pinks and creams. Pictures of Carrie's son and daughter—both in uniform—crowd tabletops in silver frames. A crib for a visiting granddaughter stands ready in the guest room.

And if that isn't Sparks-y enough for you, Carrie runs her own business selling antique furniture—and actually makes a living at it.

Bet you're thinking transplanted New York City designer with a fine arts degree, right? Or perhaps she's a fictional character?

Are you kidding? Carrie is a retired Navy wife who followed her husband around the country for twenty-five years. She doesn't have a degree in fine arts and she's never spent much time in NYC. But Carrie has managed to do the very thing that most of us go crazy trying to do. She has found meaningful work despite the needs of the military.

Learning to "make much of many littles" was one Carrie Goodman's strategies. As a stay-at-home mom, Carrie always made her house her hobby—painting, stenciling, hunting antiques. When her kids went to school, she and another Navy wife started an antique store in Jacksonville, Florida. It was her first business. She had to sell the business when she moved, but she got other jobs and started other businesses—all of which had something to do with home decorating. Stenciling walls and fabric, working at a furniture and gift shop—Carrie's done it all, even wallpapering most of northern Virginia.

"I could always take it with me," said Carrie. "And as styles changed, I was able to change with them."

When she and her husband settled in Virginia Beach, Carrie became an antiques dealer in Williamsburg and then moved her business when the market changed.

"You have to tap into your interests," says Carrie. "You can take advantage of your surroundings and what you are exposed to."

But what if I can't stencil? What if pasting up a wallpaper border is the extent of my decorating ability? Well, creative fields aren't the only ones that move easily. Many spouses are finding jobs they can do online that don't depend on showing up from nine to five every day. Think outside the box.

Finding meaningful work—and the paycheck it delivers—is one of the things that makes military life a little more bearable. And that's no work of fiction.

At Long Last, Liberty

It's an unwritten rule among Homefront Clubbers *never* to wish our husbands out to sea. It isn't that we won't let ourselves forget how tough a deployment can be. We can and we do. It isn't that our husbands are perfect saints. Believe me, they're not.

It's just a longing to hang on to our priceless time together as a family—even when there seems to be an awful lot of it.

One summer we had way too much togetherness. Every weekend, Brad would ask me what I wanted to do. Every weekend, I'd suggest going to the beach. Every weekend, he would complain about the four hours of Delaware beach traffic. And every weekend I'd want to squish his head.

On the very last decent beach weekend, I woke up and declared that I was going to the beach. Without him.

"Oh," he said, faintly incredulous. "I guess I'm staying here? With the kids?"

"No, I'll take Kelsey. She likes the beach as much as I do. And *she* never complains about traffic."

He wasn't that happy. Nor was he jumping into the car to go to the beach.

Several hours later, my eight-year-old and I sauntered over the board-walk at Cape Henlopen beach—and my heart promptly dropped. The beach was so crowded. Wall-to-wall people. But it was Brad who hated a crowded beach, not me.

My daughter and I dove into the surf beside a group that sported more tattoos than good sense. The salt prickled my skin and dripped from my hairline, stinging my eyes until it felt like I'd been crying all week. I meant to relax, be happy, enjoy myself. But I couldn't shake feeling guilty and selfish for leaving the guys at home. We *never*—I mean *never*—spent weekends apart. Shouldn't I have waited for the day when Brad would finally want to come too?

During sea duty, every day that Brad was home from the ship was rare and precious. We doled those days out stingily to our parents and friends, hoarding them for our little family to share. But the shore tour gave us thirty-nine consecutive weekends together. Enough weekends that waking up on Saturday morning with the delicious tickle of his breath on my neck no longer qualified as an Act of God.

At last we were sated, we had had enough. That thirst for togetherness was quenched. Other needs became apparent—like my need to be free, to indulge in what *I* want to do, to have liberty.

That day, Kelsey and I hunted purple-tipped shells, drank frozen lemonade, sketched with colored pencils. We swam until we lost the day; the sky and water turned suddenly gray. We stopped at Subway for dinner—because Brad hates Subway.

We arrived home to find Sam sound asleep and Brad cozy in bed with his canoe catalogues. I pounced, joyfully kissing him, burying my face in his neck, feeling his arm curve around my waist, his lips in my hair.

"Had a good time, did you?" he asked.

I nodded happily and we soon settled in for the long night's rest. I drifted off, still feeling the ebb and flow of the tide on my legs, carrying me forward, carrying me back. And I wished for both of us to stay right here. Forever.

4 Separation

Where Oh Where Are You Tonight?

Where oh where are you tonight?
Why did you leave me here all alone?
I searched the world over and thought I found true love.
You joined the Navy and pfffft you were gone.

—Traditional Navy wife tune as adapted from *Hee Haw*

I'VE GOT PLENTY OF THINGS to worry about when I turn off the light. Why the elastic waistband on my pajama pants is tight. How long it will take our Little Tikes cabin to decompose in the landfill. Why my middle schooler is so hot to shop at Sluts "Я" Us.

What I don't have to worry about is Vlad the Impaler and his chums crossing the border, pillaging my village, and generally taking over the government while I sleep. Invasion is just not my worry. It's one more reason to love all those men and women in uniform.

Yet as grateful as I am to be Vlad-free, being married to one of the guys who protects and serves does have certain drawbacks: namely, that my husband keeps getting sent overseas to train, complete missions, and strive for world peace. Go figure. Like the guy isn't capable of doing all that right here at home whilst gripping a ham sandwich in one hand and the baby seat in the other.

No matter how multitaskable all our service members are, the Pentagon persists in sending them far, far away to do their jobs. They like to call the whole exercise a deployment, a float, a mobilization, a pump, or an unaccompanied tour.

And you won't like it. Really, you won't. No matter how hard you try to love that deployment and invite it right on in for dinner, it still has a way of leaving a real mess behind it. Deployment is a notoriously bad houseguest. Especially when it's unexpected.

Some June Cleavers still cling to the idea that if we at home just keep busy enough, the deployment will be nothing but "a minor inconvenience." I'll warn you right now, those are the kind of women who will tell you (when your husband has been gone for seven-and-a-half months and their husbands are in the backyard fertilizing the lawn) they secretly wish their husband would deploy. Me too.

While I strongly recommend you do not belt these women (even if they are your blood relations), the urge to do so is perfectly normal. It may help to tell yourself that perhaps Ward is not such a good kisser. Perhaps Ward does not fold laundry. Perhaps Ward spits when he talks and June does not suffer when he is away.

But, mercy, I do. You probably do too. Or will, when he's gone. And that's not such a bad thing. We live in a society in which people think any kind of pain is bad and should be stopped instantly. Take a pill. Get a vaccination. No matter how much it hurts this minute, deployment isn't a catastrophic kind of pain. As much as you don't want to, you will get through it. That terrible ache in your throat, that sting in your eyes, that feeling you get every time you open your beloved's closet simply means that you have something to lose. You have someone worth missing. Truly, you are the lucky one.

A Test of Your Womanhood

Over the past few years, I have learned to think of a deployment not as a tragedy, and certainly not as a minor inconvenience, but as a test of my womanhoooooood. You've got to say it that way: womanhoooooood. Deployment, more than achievement at work or in school, more than pregnancy, even more than a bad case of mastitis, will teach you just how much of a woman you are. It will teach you where the edge is and just how far you can teeter there without falling into an entire case of Fudgsicles.

All of us Homefront Clubbers manage to get through it somehow.

The question is: How? The answer is: Any way we can—without drugs, without booze, without sex, without rock 'n' roll. Well, maybe the kabash on the rock 'n' roll is a bit too much. Let's just say that as long as you hold firm on the drugs, booze, and sex thing, you can turn up the volume all you want. See, I like you. And Springsteen; I really like Springsteen.

Aside from playing heavy doses of the Boss, you really ought to know that there is no regulation requiring you to feel like a hero or a cheerleader when your spouse deploys—even if he is deploying during wartime. There is no need for you to drape yourself in red, white, and blue and chat about how you are glad to do your part for the country. You don't have to agree with the politics that send him away. You don't have to act like you're happy he's gone.

All you're required to do is to behave like a woman; hold firm to the vows of your marriage and the responsibilities of parenthood. And you were going to do that anyway.

What You Control

Deployment is a pass/fail exercise. You make it to the end of the pier, the runway, the arrival gate—or you don't. The key to getting through is grasping the fact that the situation is out of your control—your spouse must deploy. You can't control what happens to him on the deployment. You can't control the date he is coming home.

That drives us crazy. Military wives tend to be a mighty organized bunch of people. We like to have control over all aspects of our lives. Deployment, however, leaps out of the box like a caffeinated monkey.

It ain't pretty.

But there are many things over which you have dominion. You can control how you react to the facts of your life. You can control the number of items you put on your to-do list. You can control your exercise and eating habits, your consumption of cigarettes and alcohol, how you raise your kids. You can control your expectations and how you treat other people.

The key is just to do it. Style is not required, though appreciated by those who have been there and done that. My husband has already deployed too many times. I cannot count the number of days and months and years we have spent apart. Considering the political climate and his orders to another seagoing unit, I expect to add more deployments to that total before I haul his stuff to the curb.

So I go boldly into deployment knowing that I'll have those days when all my major appliances seem possessed. I'll have to change flat tires. I'll miss my dental appointment for the fourth time and the dentist will yell at me. I'll even have days where I have failed at what I was supposed to do. But I am a hardheaded woman. I bend and do not bow. I'm just glad I have plenty of company.

Predeployment

Workups and Other Things That Cause Wrinkles

Although the rest of the world may divide military spouses into officer and enlisted groups, those of us living the life know we are actually divided into two more serious groups:

1. Those driven insane by the never-ending nature of deployments.

2. Those driven insane by all the in/out-duty-night-never-plan-a-blessed-thing rest of the time. Also referred to as "workups."

To the masters of the fleet and battalion, workups must seem like a sound idea. For four or five months before a scheduled deployment, Army and Marine units get sent to the field to fire their weapons, drive their vehicles, and generally practice their appointed missions. Navy crews go to sea to test the plant and make sure the engines will make it all the way to Gibraltar. They all get the chance to run an operation or two, sleep up to four hours at a time, drive those little boats out of the back of the amphibious ships, and gather up Marines and all their equipment. Neat-o!

Visit the Unit

Before the unit deploys, it helps to see where your husband is going to be working and eating, and who he is going to be working and eating with. If your unit hasn't already planned an event for families that includes ship and aircraft tours, suggest it to your ombudsman or key spouse.

To them, workups make sense. But to us practical folks at home, workups seem to make about as much sense as driving the Winnebago to Wapakoneta, Ohio, and back as a test drive for next fall's trip to the Grand Canyon. Wouldn't a three-hour tour around the pier do just as much good?

Little do they know that while they are busy working up, we spouses at home are starting to collect all the crazy-making reminders that deployment is just around the corner. Friends forget exactly which day our husbands are deploying, so they ask and ask and ask again. Kids want to know how many days Daddy will be home and will that be enough time to buy a dwarf hamster? Acquaintances advise us that the unit won't be gone that long. Then, someone invariably delivers the clincher, "It will all be over before you know it."

Right. Is it any wonder that during the workup period I take to tucking a Marlboro behind my left ear?

I can see how the drawn-out nature of the workup is well suited to building dread in the most stalwart of souls. Workups are Christmas sales the day after Thanksgiving. The senior prom before graduation. Back-to-school displays in July. That itching you get in the back of your throat just before you come down with the flu.

Workups are the signal to all military families that a change—and not a welcome one—is about to begin.

To-Do Lists *Not* To Do

Just after the workups stop, and about a month before deployment hits, my husband starts hearing some mysterious inner alarm clock. This alarm tells him that now is the time to get his winter uniforms striped. To call his sister for an hour to say good-bye before he leaves. To shop for basketball shoes with his daughter, hit a bucket of balls with his son, and paint the trim in the living room so his wife will think of him fondly in the wee small hours.

It is the one alarm clock I would most like to smack down. Violently. Because every time he ticks something off of his list of things-to-do-before-I-deploy, I find myself adding and adding and adding to my lists of things-to-do-after-he-goes. And I do mean lists. While he's working so hard to leave me, I'm defiantly making lists of all the reasons I will be glad that he is gone. *(I will sleep with all his pillows. Every sweatshirt he leaves in the closet is officially community property. We will not listen to Perry Como for 180 straight days.)*

I list things I will do to work off the anxiety of those first three weeks. *(Scrub the kitchen floor. Sort all the Tupperware so that every container and lid are reunited. Take kids to Ben & Jerry's every day.)*

I even make lists of lists-I-must-not-make. *(Reasons why I will cry when he is gone. Reasons why the kids will want their dad. Major holidays and birthdays he will not attend. Bad things that just might happen.)*

Just as my predeployment lists tower above me, threatening to crash down over us all, I send the whole family straight to bed. Because the predeployment period is a time to live simply. A time to get enough sleep, try really hard not to pick a fight, order pizzas, put off projects. It's

Visit the Family

Before deployment, it is customary to go back home to visit family and friends. Try to schedule this four or more weeks before the actual deployment date, preferably more. Although his parents may prefer to wait until the week before he leaves, or even to see the unit off, this is too stressful for deploying families. Avoid the fight. Draw a box around the last two weeks your service member will be at home and keep it for spouses and children only. See chapter 7 for more suggestions for dealing with in-laws.

With a Little Help from Your Friends

No one surfs the deployment alone. I find I always need at least three people who do not know each other to be my friends during a deployment. None of them can be a man and at least one must have no connection to military life.

One to Go and Do with You

Even if you work and/or have kids, deployment leaves you with a lot of empty hours that other people fill with family activities. Find someone who has the same empty Sunday afternoons. Go to the movies, take the kids to the park, or attend a yoga class. This is the ideal role for another wife from the command, even if you don't have much in common.

One to Console You

Everyone needs a friend who will listen to her heart. Someone who can stand to hear how your beloved is missing your anniversary. Or how sick you are of the deployment. Or how the e-mail is down again. This friend must swear to end every conversation by reminding you that your husband is a really good guy and you are lucky to have each other. Mothers are often very good at this role. Fellow members of the command are not.

One to Kick You in the Head

Sometimes, we go overboard with the daily pity party. Get yourself a friend who won't put up with too much goo. Find someone who will remind you of your blessings, despite the deployment, and tell you to Get Over It. An older friend,

a time to let ourselves be lulled by the Big Snooze that comes before he has to leave.

The alarm shrieks constantly: The deployment is coming! The deployment is coming! But we have to turn it off, smack it down, roll into each other's arms. And wait until tomorrow.

Deployment

Tell Me the Secret

Some women seem to know the secret to getting through a deployment pain free. I fear I am simply not one of them. I have seen those chicks in action. During my husband's first cruise, I knew this one senior-wife type who drove a shiny blue Volvo station wagon, shopped only at Talbots, and dressed her little blonde daughters in patent-leather shoes. Despite the deployment, she always looked like she had never had a bad day in her life.

I, on the other hand, was a Poor Unfortunate. I was twenty-three, literally dying of lovesickness, joblessness, friendlessness.

At a ship party, I sidled up to Volvo Lady, as though being near her would put me in reach of The Secret. She was telling her friends how she had just found matching Barbie Christmas campers for her girls.

Noticing me lurking there, Volvo Lady smiled and asked, "How are you, dear?"

I was young enough and hurting enough to think this was an actual question. So I blurted out, "I can't stand the loneliness, can you? I can hardly sleep. The days last so long. It's like Alaskan winter here, where the sun doesn't shine for twenty-four hours straight, isn't it? I'm cultivating friends on the West Coast because I figure when it's midnight here, it's only 9 o'clock there, and that isn't too late to call . . ."

My voice trailed off. Volvo Lady and her friends stared at me as if I might self-destruct right there on the pier. We don't bare souls in the Navy.

But I was a girl who was awake every night, watching whatever was on after Conan O'Brien, a girl who slept with the TV muttering to itself until morning, and a lamp glowing bravely at my bedside. "I just wanted to know," I whispered, "how do you do it?"

neighbor, or sister who understands the military but is not associated with the command can fill this role.

You don't know enough people to fit the bill? Work is a good place to meet them; your apartment is not. Moms meet other moms at playgroups or at the playground. People make friends at support group meetings, ship picnics, Weight Watchers, Starbucks. Personally, I'm shy. But when you need new friends, you gotta be workin' it all the time. Start now.

Perfect silence reigned. At the time, I thought it was because Volvo Lady and her friends thought I was so utterly hopeless. So inept. So close to being voted Most Likely Not to Be a Navy Wife This Time Next Year.

But now that I've done my cruises, picked up the bits of Barbie's stupid camper, and buckled my own kids into any pair of matching shoes for command parties, I don't believe Volvo Lady was thinking I was overly weird. Now, I'd put money on the fact that she was at a loss for words to describe exactly how she made it through all those deployments.

In Michael Cunningham's book *The Hours,* which was made into an Oscar-nominated movie, all of the characters are slugging through the tedious hours of their lives in one way or another. And they aren't even in the military.

In the book, characters whose lives appear so seamless on the outside are actually filled with worry. That something was wrong with the ring they gave their daughter on her eighteenth birthday. That the message on a birthday cake is off center. That they are shallow and boring and not quite the geniuses they wish they were. These characters get through hours of pain and tedium to get to the minutes of happiness and fulfillment.

I wish Mr. Cunningham had gotten on the ball with this concept years earlier (but then maybe Nicole Kidman wouldn't have been available for the role). Because I'm sure this really is what the Volvo Lady wanted to tell me. That this party was one of her minutes of happiness. That when it was over, her daughters would be sticky and their shoes would be scuffed and the perfect-looking little girls would probably slap each other on the way home.

That each night she tells herself she only has to get through until dinner, until the girls are in bed, until Conan O'Brien comes on again.

I don't know that my twenty-three-year-old self could have understood that concept. I probably would have railed against the idea that there are some hours in life you just get through. At the time, I thought we were duty bound to be present for joy at every minute. That loneliness was somehow wrong.

But now I can accept that during some hours of a deployment, you are not required to be fully self-actualized. During some of the hours of a deployment, you are allowed to just get through. And while you're just getting through, you keep reminding yourself that sometimes all of the traffic lights will be green. And sometimes you will rock a crying baby to sleep at your breast. And sometimes you will wake with rain on the window and your love in your arms and it won't be your turn for deployment anymore.

Get through the hours. And the happy minutes will come.

Realistic Goals

I'm married to a guy who truly believes that a loving way to get the deployment off to a good start is discussing the Importance of Setting Personal Goals. No kisses or kind compliments for us, just True Love through Personal Goal Setting.

In addition to the Pentagon-wide goal of "Vanquish Thine Enemy," my husband's most recent recital of deployment goals included negotiating orders, sending good Christmas gifts, expanding his career knowledge through experience and books, losing weight, and working out daily with a Marine whose tattooed forearms render him capable of taking on Bluto.

That's a lot to accomplish for a man in a profession without leisure hours. But I know him. My husband will surely sail home with enemies vanquished (or well on their way to vanquishment), a chiseled jawline, conversation full of the intimate details of why Admiral Lord Nelson was such a weird guy, and, I fear, a set of forearms that have thickened three sizes since our last Farewell.

That would all be well and good. What's more delightful than a marital partner who sets and reaches goals, right? Of course, right. Right up until you read his innocently phrased next question, "So what are your goals for the deployment?"

My goals?

Everyone, from my mother to the pamphlet writers down at the Family Support Center, seem to be eagerly awaiting my plans. Surely I have hours now available which I used to waste doing husband-tending things like cooking dinner, picking up dry cleaning, or snuggling in the lap of my beloved. According to the recognized wisdom of the day, deployment is the time for Little Military Spouse Me to reawaken my previously neglected personal goals.

Darn tootin'.

I enjoy pondering my old favorites—like my goal to return to a single-digit dress size (last achieved when my age was also written in a single digit). My goal to walk the fat dog daily—burning calories and preventing wet patches on the carpet at the same time. My goal to paint those baseboards my husband didn't get around to. Get Christmas packages in the mail by November 1. Tile the kitchen floor with adobe tiles crafted and fired from clay dug in the backyard. Sew a king-size quilt with a pictorial display of the most important historical events of the twentieth century. In velvet.

But I know me. I will do none of these things. Two weeks before my beloved gets home, I will be stricken with the knowledge that I am, in fact, a slug. The conquering hero is sure to sweep in with his newly defined jawline and taut forearms and shipshape career to find that the very Fritos crumbs that were peeking out from under the dishwasher the day he left are still there. That the dog still waddles. That I only got to the ripping-up-the-kitchen-floor stage and have been living with the demolition ever since.

I am not the only one at this slugfest. In surveys of other spouses, I've found that the problem lies with the goals themselves, not with the sluggishness of the particular goal setter. We spouses—parents in particular—forget that all the "extra" hours we supposedly gain during sea time also come with "extra" chores to fill them.

So the next time your guy deploys, I suggest dashing off a different list of personal goals. Make it a more humble list, a smaller list, a list without glory. Simply resolve to take on all the things that he is, all the jobs that he does.

My own new list will include such glamorous goals as remembering to take the trash to the curb on Sunday nights. Cleaning up the kitchen after dinner. Mowing the lawn at least once. Putting the children to bed the way he does, with stories and prayers and patience. Shooting free throws. And, perhaps, achieving rapture in a minivan as my gluteus maximus becomes one with the seat.

If I can do all this while he's gone, I'll be very proud. Really, I will. Even as I'm shoving those last Frito crumbs back under the dishwasher.

The Wonders of E-Mail

I'm not a great defender of the Dot.commers or Generation Xers or whatever those post–high school/pre-mortgage types are calling themselves these days. I had to take offense on their behalf, though, when it was reported a while back that the sailors on the USS *Enterprise* (average age nineteen and a half) threw back their heads and roared whenever the e-mail went down.

The salty dogs on the carrier claimed that these youngsters are technologically spoiled, too used to instant access, and have no idea what it is like to wait two or three weeks for a letter. You almost expected one of them to hitch up his pants and grumble, "Back in the old days . . ."

Pffffft on the old days. Count me in with the Dot.commers. My husband and I have had only one deployment with the benefit of e-mail access. It is everything I ever dreamed of. It's like French fries instead of hardtack on the mess deck. Direct deposit instead of pieces of eight. Hot showers instead of keelhauling.

On our first deployment, I wrote letters to my husband on a ream of love-red paper. I tucked the epistles into matching red envelopes too. I wanted those guys in the mail room to know that someone in the world gave a damn about this junior-junior-junior guy—even if it was only me. Drama, after all, is my forte.

I poured my heart out every night and waited weeks for the mail to come. On the rare day when I actually got a letter from the ship, Dan-Dan-the-Nice-Postman would ring the doorbell so I could fling myself out on the steps and rip open the only words I had from my husband.

But my Dear One is not one of those men who express themselves beautifully on paper. Or easily. Or often. In one instance, I found he had let twenty-eight days go by without putting pen to paper, ear to phone, thought to feelings about his little wife across the water.

Men can do that kind of stuff.

Back then the familiar handwriting on the page was more comforting than the things he wrote. I envied my sister-in-law, who received free morale calls from her Air Force husband. We were just grateful when sailor phones installed on the ship meant short, but weekly, phone calls. Cell phones, unfortunately, have a funny way of not working across large bodies of water.

I didn't expect e-mail to make that much of a difference to us or to other military families. But it has. There must be something about e-mail, as opposed to letters, or even phone calls, that's particularly comfortable for men. While their words on paper seemed squeezed out, as if they had to raise their hands and ask how to spell everything, e-mail seems to free their hands. On most days, I got actual paragraphs about whether I remembered to start his car. (Oops.) Why he was glad the Yankees won the pennant (they did?). How he wished he were home in autumn because he likes to see me in sweaters (don't ask). Even on his worst days, he would write, "Three hours of sleep. Love you." Nuff said.

The communication between us hasn't improved simply because he's older now, more mature, and far more thoughtful than he was during the Cruise of the Love-Red Letters. Cards from him still have the same three phrases on them: Love you. Miss you. Wish you were here.

It is the blessed dailiness of e-mail that keeps us together, as if we were sitting across from each other at the dining room table. E-mail makes it okay to tell the bad stuff that happens, explain how things work, compliment and complain, pine for each other, and sort out the details of raising children and owning a home and sharing a life together.

Although it can be done in letters, and certainly was done that way in the past, the intimacy of the immediate keeps you feeling much closer. And truly, that happens best in the embrace of an e-mail. Which is all very well if you can afford to own a computer. Or if you are part of a command that has e-mail capability. Or if your battalion is not in the field. Or if you have access to a workstation, not just a rack and a seabag. And, of course, if the e-mail is actually up and running.

So are those of us with e-mail access to our deployed ones spoiled? Absolutely. Could we go back to the old way if we had to? Sure, just like we could go back to doing laundry with a wringer or picking up dust mites without a Swiffer, or snapping on undergarments that claim not a thread of Lycra. Hey, we're not totally without character.

But e-mail is so sweet. It is the illusion that we are still on the same page on the same day. It is the confidence that we are still a team, though a disembodied one. It is a reason to put into words every day *why* I miss you and what I miss about you and not just *that* I miss you at all. And it's just about free. What's not to love?

How Do I Love Thee? Let Me Call and Count the Ways

Agree to agree. Some sailors send their wives a letter every day. Scented, embossed, illustrated letters actually written on paper. Others think about you every now and then and send a letter once during the entire float. It doesn't really matter. The important thing is that you agree how much and how often you are going to communicate—before your husband deploys.

Know the ups and downs of cell phones. Cell phones are a great way to keep in touch when your service member is close to a cell phone tower—and relatively inexpensive with the right calling plan. But they don't work over large bodies of water. And commands often require the troops to turn off their phones while in the field to limit compromising the mission. Know the pros and cons of cell phones so you won't be disappointed.

Limit other phone use. The telephone is, of course, the next best thing to being there. But it can bleed you dry. And it is *so* easy to fight on the phone. When a Marine or soldier is in the field, he is tired, hot, dirty, and irritable. It's easy for him to say something he doesn't mean—then get frustrated about spending fifty bucks while you give him the silent treatment. Try to arrange for a particular time during the week for him to call. Agree in advance on how many minutes you will talk. Plan something pleasant to discuss.

Don't use e-mail for tasking. E-mail is a blessing, but many wives say their husbands get into the habit of using it only for tasking. You know, the whole honey-did-you-check-the-oil thing. Make it a rule that for every task he gives you in an e-mail, he must tell you something he missed about you that day.

Send packages. Married to a young guy? *Send food!* Home-baked goods are the food of choice, but the mail system can be chancy. Send something homemade but include a bag of Oreos or Cheez-Its in case the snickerdoodles don't make it. And tuck a note in along with the goodies. Something that's come from your hand and your home means the world to a guy on deployment. Service members say they read and reread everything from home, over and over again.

Participate in those goofy support-group projects. The little craft projects the support group makes for Halloween may seem very, very goofy to you. Yet the guys like them. Strange, but true. It makes them feel better to see your signature on a sign or a pair of funny socks that you made. He won't push you to do it, he won't even mention it, but it does add a little to his status. Every little thing matters.

Spirituality

The one deployment skill I ought to reach for more often is the one that reads: Renew spiritual life.

Because it can be such a time of trial, many military spouses report that deployment was a spiritual turning point for them. They found that they prayed more, read the Bible more, became more conscious of their relationship with God. I mean to be that way too. But somehow, my prayers generally run along the line of, "Lord, let there be an e-mail." Or, "Thank

A Place of Your Own

Were you the kind of kid who played under the dining room table? Made tents in the backyard? Preferred a camper to your actual house? It turns out that our preference for small enclosed places is natural. It makes us feel safer—an important part of getting through deployment.

"Smaller, more cozy places evoke a sense of security and introspection," says architect Sarah Susanka, author of *The Not So Big House*. Resolve to spend a little time in the smaller, cozier areas of your home.

heavens this day is over." Somehow, I don't think this is the kind of prayerful reflection that the Lord has in mind for me. Or for anyone else either.

But that doesn't mean we shouldn't try. Even if you haven't been a terribly religious person in the past, resolve to actively look for a congregation you feel comfortable in.

Complaining

Everyone handles deployment differently. I cry; heck, I sob. I beat pillows and boo-hoo to beat the band. Then I get over it. Take a nice shower, move on. I think that's pretty normal.

My best friend, Dawn, is different. She cleans when her husband is deployed. Until eleven o'clock at night. Until the grout gleams. Until she's just so tired of cleaning, she can pretend she doesn't notice her husband is gone. It's her way.

Our neighbor, who declares deployments are no big deal, flies off the handle over nothing when her husband's gone. She ends up taking her deployment frustration out by flaming on unsuspecting plumbers and school secretaries. It's scary. We may post a danger sign in her driveway.

Still other women handle separation by eating or by forgetting to eat. By talking on the phone. By working extra hours. By scheduling every possible minute. By watching scandalous amounts of TV. It would be great if our reactions to deployment and separation were predictable so we could at least understand each other. But that would be too easy, wouldn't it?

Perhaps the biggest difference among us is the way we deal with our complaints. Susan, whose husband has been enlisted for seventeen years, got fed up with complainers during the war in Iraq.

"I have lost a lot of my patience for whining from grown people about the Navy," Susan said. "It is not good for anyone to deal with pain alone. Talking is the best solution, but there is talking and there is whining."

True. But complainers sometimes do a bit of both. I think some complainers are simply the type of people who need to think out loud before they come up with a solution to their problems.

I am just that kind of complainer, I know. I'm such a whiner, I'm practically colicky. Ask anyone. For me, solving a problem is just like getting dinner on the table. First, I have to actually fold and put away the clean laundry that has piled on the table until it touches the light fixture. (It's a very low light fixture. Honest.) Then, I have to toss out a week's worth of newspapers. Find a different spot for the sewing machine. Stow backpacks. Throw away irreplaceable papers.

Only then can I think about dinner. As in, "Gee, this table looks so nice, I don't want to mess it up. Let's go out for dinner."

The same goes for my problems when my husband is gone. First, I have to moan about how I can't make any plans for the summer, since I don't know when he's getting back. Then, I have to complain that I haven't had a steak all year, since I don't know how to light the grill. Then, I have to suffer out loud over a life spent waiting on someone else. Wah. Wah. Wah.

At about this point, it occurs to me (perhaps because my friends brandish baseball bats in my direction) that it is Time to Act. I decide to make summer plans so that they can be changed if the ship gets home early. I ask my neighbor to teach me to light the grill. I learn how to use mascara to cover my burnt eyelashes. I scrub my kitchen floor.

Susan says when it comes to complaining, finding the *right* person to talk to is key. "Talking to a friend that is connected to the command or the ombudsman or the key spouse would be a good first step. They are in the same boat and can understand a little better what you might be dealing with because every command is different and every cruise is different."

Susan suggests you approach the command master chief's spouse or the command sergeant major's spouse if you can't talk to anyone else. I think that families (officer or enlisted) can go to other experienced command spouses, like the chaplain's spouse, the executive officer's spouse, or the commanding officer's spouse. Many of them (though, not all) are great resources. They can't solve your problems, but they'll know where to direct you, or they can find out.

Maybe we complainers ought to realize, too, that misery is a communicable disease—especially within a command. Don't let appearances deceive you. When they are deep into a deployment, everyone in the command is as worn down as you. It helps to cultivate a friendship with the kind of woman outside the military who has the energy to listen—and will tell you that the pity party is over. (See "One to Kick You in the Head" in the sidebar on page 74.)

In our community, the difference between complaining and talking seems to come down to action. Yes, into all lives a little self-pity must fall. Talk about it all you want. But when we choose to act, that's when we prove ourselves the women we want to be. Keep fighting the good fight.

Self-Sufficiency

For most military spouses, the actual day-to-day life of a deployment is no big deal. We handle everything we ever handled before our spouses deployed, perhaps more. We shrug it off. What chore at home could possibly compare to doing maintenance on an amphibious assault vehicle in the desert? What could be worse than dodging sniper fire? How

Physical Symptoms

Deployment feels terrible for everyone. However, if you find yourself exhibiting the physical symptoms of stress—such as eczema, psoriasis, hair loss, or insomnia—it's time to get some help. Call your ombudsman and a doctor. They won't get your husband sent home, but they will get you the kind of help you need.

could driving to San Jose in heavy traffic compare to flying sorties over Baghdad in the dark?

Compared to our spouses, we live the good life. We sleep in our own beds. And as long as everything goes perfectly well, everything goes perfectly well.

Fate has plans for military spouses, though. Just when we get to thinking that deployment is no big deal and we could quite possibly overrun a small country on our own, the dishwasher breaks, a library book disappears, and a check bounces. On the same day. Suddenly, we're standing back and watching ourselves dissolve into tears over *nothing*.

Thus, deployment doth make spigots of us all.

During one deployment, when I was seven months pregnant, I sort of fainted and fell in a parking lot. The medical determination was that I couldn't gestate and drive my daughter to three swim practices and three basketball games a week. My eleven-year-old had to quit one of her activities.

I fell apart. No one could understand it. My daughter was happy to concentrate on basketball. The swim team people were reasonable. Every other sports parent secretly envied me.

But I took it as a sign of my own personal doom. Not driving to swim practice meant I couldn't keep up with the deployment. I was destined to fall behind the wagon train. It meant I'd end up pushing my children in a wheelbarrow with my palms blistering and my bloody stumps mussing the trail behind me. Next stop: Donner Pass.

Yet, what did it really mean? Nothing. It meant I was going to have a baby. That our family would change. We could handle it.

We military moms have got to learn to be easier on ourselves during deployment—as if. We've still got to remember that deployment breakdowns mean . . . nothing. Cry all you want. It's just your heart's signal that emotionally you've had enough for that day. You'll get up and do some more tomorrow. Because tomorrow is another day.

Asking for Help

My girlfriend stopped at the red light and cast me a sidelong glance. "Are you going to do that all afternoon?"

"Do what?"

Fidelity

If this is your first deployment, I'm sure some people have already tried to scare you with stories of Noah's Ark Syndrome. That's the one in which the entire crew or detachment is supposed to pair off as soon as they pull away from the pier. This happens—generally among the young single people. Married people who claim that this is common have done it themselves. A special level of hell has been reserved just for them. Don't join them. Nothing will scar your young marriage worse than infidelity. This is a time to bolster your same-sex, platonic friendships. Be true to each other. Love matters. Love lasts.

"Hang your head out the window that way. You look like you ought to be wearing a bandanna around your furry black neck and sniffing the seats for stray chip crumbs. People are staring."

"So I'm a little excited to be in the car again," I said, turning around in my seat three times and showing my teeth to a Pomeranian in the white Bronco in the next lane. "So what?"

"So what?" she huffed. "So you should be asking for help. Nobody but you expects you to do everything yourself. You've got a newborn baby and your husband is deployed and you've got 149 stitches or something. I can drive you wherever you need to go. You can just call and . . ."

"Yeah, yeah, yeah," I mumbled, leaning my chin into the back draft. Get help. Get help. That's what everyone has been saying to me since I was prohibited from driving for the four weeks following a C-section. It about killed me.

Not the C-section. It just killed me to be forced to ask my friends and neighbors to drive my kids to school or pick up a gallon of milk and some Nacho Cheese Doritos at the grocery. Ugh. Couldn't do it. Would much rather have spent my time crawling through a hurricane with the squalling baby strapped to my back, hauling home the dry cleaning.

Why? Because I'm an idiot, that's why.

Now, I can easily see why *other* people have the right to ask for help. I'm always delighted to jump in with a ride to soccer here, free babysitting there, and the healing power of lasagna everywhere else. When I read about some farmer whose son is having brain surgery during harvest time, and who refuses help from his neighbors, I can't understand that behavior at all. My heavens, that guy needs combines and trailers and folks who know what alfalfa looks like. If I needed a combine, believe me, I'd be the first to ask for help.

So why is it so hard for me to accept and ask for help when so many kind people offer it every day? One of my neighbors says that when you let people help, you really are doing them a favor. It feels good to help someone else. I can see that. Giving when I don't expect to receive is no problem. Receiving when I cannot possibly give back makes me feel like I've got the mark of Cain inscribed on my forehead.

When it is my own family, I'm more comfortable asking for and receiving help. I fantasize that my parents will give up their silly notion that they have to conduct their own lives in placid Ohio and move right in with me instead. They are allowed to do my laundry and mow my lawn and administer lasagna to their hearts' content. With them, I understand the circle of giving from parent to child to parent to child.

It may take more character and insight than I've got to see that same circle of giving working in the rest of the world. The line is so much longer than it is in a family, so much more tenuous. But that doesn't

Kids and Deployment

It usually happens after one child has brought home a D for the science project she didn't finish and the other got a punch in the nose for running around with his brother's underpants on his head. That's when you invariably hear them crying for their deployed parent.

It's tempting to talk them out of it. Don't. I've found it works best when I agree with them. I say, "Yes, you miss your dad." "Yes, it's stupid that he's gone." "Yes, honey, it hurts." I back this up at calmer times by reminding my kids of all the good things about their dad and how much he loves them, even if he isn't here. It really works. (See chapter 6 for more tips on kids and separation.)

The Mark

They say that during deployment the mark of a smart woman is being able to accept help. And the mark of a strong woman is being able to ask for it.

mean it isn't there. Someday, I will drive a new mom to her first doctor's appointment, the way my friend did for me. Someday, I will drop off sub sandwiches and chocolate ice cream pie to a hungry family, the way my friend did for me. Someday, I will e-mail digital pictures of a newborn to a new dad half a world away, the way my friend did for me.

Until then, I will have to sit back and receive with a gracious heart—and pretend it isn't killing me.

Pre-Homecoming

At some blessed, unspecified moment during the deployment, you will become aware that the wait is almost at an end. Sometimes it happens when a major hurdle or holiday has passed. Sometimes, when you turn the last page of the calendar. Sometimes, when you realize that the dirty laundry has taken over the basement and has started encroaching on the stairs.

Just because the deployment is nearly over does not mean you are feeling fine and dandy, although you do have your dandy days. Here are a few of the things you need to know about the pre-homecoming period.

Patience

patience, n.: a minor form of despair, disguised as a virtue.
—Ambrose Bierce, *The Devil's Dictionary*

I would have made a very bad cow. Standing outside in the rain, lumbering under trees to find shade—the life of the average cow seems to be largely about waiting. I'm not good at waiting. Born without patience, I am the kind of woman whose watched pots never boil, whose babies seem to arrive at the eleventh month, whose not-quite-cooked turkey poisons her closest friends every year.

When it comes to having patience, I'm doomed. I do keep trying, though. My beloved fourth-grade teacher (who played Bobby Goldsboro tunes on her autoharp whenever it rained) swore that the reason we were put on earth was to learn specific lessons—different lessons for different souls. She said some of us are born to learn how to love. Others are here to learn Peacemaking 101. Still others have been sent to dwell on planet Earth until they can sing in tune with an autoharp.

Me, I'm here to wait. My divine spark has been channeled right here for the express purpose of learning to wait patiently. Not gonna happen. No matter how many times the cosmos presents me with the same lesson in patience, I never do get it.

The best I have managed so far is this dogged perseverance, which is not quite the same thing. If perseverance is X-ing out the days left of deployment, patience is being fully present in every moment before Homecoming. Patience means relishing the spread of cosmetics all over the sink. Patience means summoning the sweetness of giving your baby a bath when he is cranky. Patience is taking the time to have one last latte with your deployment friends.

So, dear cosmos, sweet universe, I promise I will keep on trying to be a patient wife and a serene mother. But I will never be a very good cow. Moo.

The Science of Waiting

Luckily for those of us who spend a lot of time waiting for the deployment to pass, the science of waiting has been greatly developed in recent years. The military isn't driving this research. Instead, it's driven by the service economy, all of those businesses—airlines, hospital emergency rooms, Disneyland—that require their customers to wait in lines. These businesses are looking for ways to make waiting seem shorter.

Scientists have discovered that unoccupied time seems longer than time spent watching TV, eating a meal, scanning tabloid headlines. Unexplained events and anxiety make a wait seem longer. Perceived unfairness makes a wait seem longer. Waiting alone is worse than waiting with companions.

The same principles hold true for deployment. If we're busy, the wait seems shorter. If they don't tell us what is going on, the wait seems longer. If a command that left after ours did get to come home early (and to our way of thinking, unfairly), the wait seems absolutely excruciating.

One of the most interesting things businesses have discovered is that consumers are happier if they're told how long they're going to have to wait—before they take their place in line. They call it the theory of prospective time. It's like seeing the sign outside the newest roller coaster announcing, "Ride two hours from this point." Or calling to get hotel reservations and hearing, "You are caller number four. Caller number one has been waiting approximately six minutes."

When you know how long the wait will be, you become the powerful one. You get to decide whether or not you have time to wait that six minutes now or whether you will hang up and call back later. We like that.

This theory of prospective time also holds true for deployments. Seems like somewhere in our minds we have set a timer for exactly six months (or whatever obnoxiously long time period our beloved is expected to be gone). The deployment that is e-x-t-e-n-d-e-d without a definite home-by date stamped prominently on the package is guaranteed to make people nutso. So what can you do?

The Incredible Expanding Deployment

Announcements that a deployment has been extended affect the troops in one of two ways. If they are being kept over there just to turn more Cheerios in the water, the guys are depressed beyond belief. But if they are being extended in the real-world sense that they will be able to use the skills they've been honing their entire adult lives, they're really, really excited. Christmas-morning excited. Fifty-yard-line-at-the-Superbowl excited.

That kind of excitement doesn't always mix well with the feeling on the Homefront. For us, a delayed Homecoming (or an unplanned departure date) is almost always a morale buster—no matter what the reason. Here are some ideas to get you through the uncertainty.

1. *Break out the little black bottle.* No matter how hard it is, if your command (not your gossipy neighbor, but the actual official

command) announces that your deployment may be extended, break out that little black bottle of White Out and wipe away all the marker lines, glitter, stars, and whirligigs you've used to demarcate Homecoming on the calendar. That probably won't be the day your ship is coming in. Another day will take its place. Accept that you'll be living with some uncertainty for the next few weeks, at least.

2. *Adopt the hardest-path contingency plan.* Not being able to adequately plan around a nonexistent schedule is one of the biggest "crazy-makers" for military spouses. Your brain scrambles in circles. If the ship gets home by the end of the month, can you still fly to your sister's wedding, move to the new duty station, sign dad up to be a peewee basketball coach? Decide that instead of ruminating, you'll plan for whichever contingency will be harder on you, more expensive, and/or more permanently scarring. That way, if your husband doesn't come home on time, you won't be disappointed. And if he does, you get the pure and perfect pleasure of having something accomplished the easy way, for once.

3. *Manage your moods.* One of the marks of a mature adult is the ability to manage his or her moods. Although we are all intimately acquainted with mood management by way of hot baths, shoe shopping, and plain and peanut M&Ms, Diane Tice, a psychologist at Case Western Reserve University, has found that these methods are less effective than when we try to cure the blues by engineering a small success. This doesn't mean losing ten pounds or running the Boston Marathon, though.

   Tice has found that the most helpful small successes are things like taking on a long-deferred small chore. Think emptying all the crumbs out of the silverware drawer, cleaning the closet under the stairs, vacuuming the layers of historical debris from the interior of the minivan. Lift your mood *and* discover lost civilizations and cup holders? Wowzer!

4. *Be remembered.* Behavioral scientists have discovered something very interesting about human beings: we have a profound fear of being forgotten. Since a heightened state of security reduces the

flow of e-mail/phone calls/solid information from your spouse, rediscover some of the old-timey ways to find out what is going on. Make sure you have completed an emergency form and contacted someone in your command—the ombudsman, the command master sergeant's spouse, or the commanding officer's spouse—to find out about support groups, phone trees, and care lines. They work.

5. *Give up all pretensions to omnipotence.* Got kids? Then you know they've always got questions they think you can answer. When is the ship coming home? Will it be Tuesday? Will Mommy be home on my birthday? Is Daddy going to come to any of my soccer games? In uncertain times, it may be tempting to threaten bodily harm to the members of your own private Spanish Inquisition. Do resist the urge. Understand this is the same group that has trouble waiting the four minutes it takes to get Easy Mac on the table.

Keep explaining that the job of military people is a lot like that of police officers and firefighters. They have to go where the action is to help people in trouble. Promise that when you know anything, they'll know it too. Encourage them to be proud of their service member—even if it means living with uncertainty for a while.

6. *Resist the urge to identify too strongly with Scarlett O'Hara.* Even though worst-case scenarios might pop into your head the moment you drift off to sleep, don't borrow trouble. It's pretty durn doubtful that we'll have a catastrophic war right here on the red earth of Tara. We probably won't be clad in yesteryear's frocks, digging around in the back forty, choking on some old radish and swearing never to be hungry or poor again. Listen only to fact, not rumor. Deal in what is probable, not possible. Don't allow yourself to watch too much TV news.

7. *Keep your perspective.* When you get fed up with all of this waiting, offer a prayer for all of the other people in our country who are waiting too. Think of couples waiting years to adopt a baby. Think of patients waiting for organ donors. Think of parents

waiting for their children to wake from comas. Waiting for our ships, planes, and platoons to come home is the kind of waiting we can definitely handle.

It's Hard to Come Home Too

Despite previous Homecomings, I never do remember to save stamina for the last grueling leg of the Iron-Woman Deployment Event. Instead, I am always the one crumpled at the side of the road, blindsided by my own fantasy life. What exactly makes me remember the last couple of weeks of the deployment as golden days of anticipation and excitement, anyway?

Instead of daydreaming about my beloved while painting welcome home signs and shopping leisurely for a floaty new dress, the reality of Homecoming is waking up in a sweat worrying. Ruminating, really. Every minute of the day.

When I confessed this to my husband a few weeks before he came home from a seven-month deployment, he wanted to know what I could possibly have to worry about this late in the game. So I wrote to him.

Dearest Husband,

These are my worries about Homecoming:

1. I'm worried you'll think I'm fat. Despite what I weigh or do not weigh, I still worry that you'll think I'm fat. It's a girl thing. Please understand.

2. I'm worried you'll forget how to understand girl things.

3. I'm worried that the kids and I will be so excited about Homecoming that we won't be able to sleep until dawn and we'll oversleep and miss Homecoming completely and you'll be the only one without a family and you'll think we don't love you.

4. I'm worried that our outfits for Homecoming will be too hot/too cold/make us look fat. (See, what did I tell you?)

5. I'm worried it will rain/snow/sleet/hail and my hair will look bad.

6. I'm worried one of the kids will fall off the pier, now that we have more kids than I have hands.

7. I'm worried you won't see the sparkling white baseboard I painted at 3 A.M. the night before you got home. Instead, I fear you'll notice the handprints, footprints, and head-shaped gouges that mark the rest of the walls.

8. I'm worried you'll like ship food more than my food.

9. I'm worried that you'll be too tired.

10. I'm worried that I'll be too tired.
11. I'm worried that the baby will take one look at your face and instantly develop colic.
12. I'm worried that instead of seeing the available lawn work as an indicator of how we love, appreciate, and can't do without you, you'll just see a scruffy lawn.
13. I'm worried you'll notice the still nearly full try-me-size can of shaving cream in the shower and suspect I haven't shaved my legs in months. Not true, mind, but I'm afraid you'll still think that.
14. I'm worried that instead of appreciating the character wrought by all those 1, 2, and 4 A.M. feedings, you'll merely note the new furrows on my face and mistake me for my mother.
15. I'm worried the dog will tell on me.
16. I'm worried that you'll be home from sea three days and then get on the phone to your detailer requesting more sea duty.

I pushed the send button on this missive and received an almost instant reply.

Dear Jace,

These are the things I worry about:

1. You don't love me as much as you remember, because I certainly love you more.

All my love and I can't wait to be a family again,

Brad

Geez, you just can't beat the rejuvenating power of the right kind of e-mail.

Homecoming

Can this marriage be saved? Although my husband and I come from the same socioeconomic background, had the same sort of schooling, and look enough alike to be brother and sister, I recently made the horrifying discovery that we come from completely different worlds when it comes to the celebration of Homecoming.

My version of Homecoming is, of course, the correct one. The children and I arrive on the pier in color-coordinated outfits à la the von Trapp family. The sun shines. The water sparkles. The gate guard waves me through to a parking place arranged in my honor. The cast of thousands parts as if we are standing on the banks of the Red Sea. The crowd cheers, "Huzzzah!" And everyone eats strawberry shortcake.

My husband's version of the perfect Homecoming is very different. In his mind's eye, he is transported via magic flue powder, or something, and arrives at the door of our home in the wee hours. He creeps from room to room, kissing the round, soft cheeks of children who have not grown up while he was gone, but gotten younger. Years younger. Brad slides into bed beside me and becomes a part of our family so seamlessly we somehow can't remember that he was ever gone. And nobody eats strawberry shortcake.

Both of us are bound to be disappointed. And not just about the strawberry shortcake. Homecoming is never what you expect.

It's a lot like Christmas. You spend months planning it, weeks sweating it. Then, you get right up to the big day and the happiness is almost obscured by all of the surrounding mess. Parking problems alone are enough to suck the joy right out of the event.

So, you do your best to keep it simple. You try to keep your expectations under control. This probably will be one of the happiest days of your life. To see his face and to hear him laugh after so many months— that part will be all you want it to be.

But this isn't all that will happen that day. The airwing will fly in an hour after its scheduled arrival. The battalion commander will want everyone to fill out some bit of paperwork before they leave. Your next-door neighbor will see your loved one walking into the house and decide to drop by to say hello—for three hours.

That's okay. Homecoming isn't perfect happiness. Homecoming isn't strawberry shortcake. But it sure beats whatever is in second place.

Stop the World, My Husband Is Home!

"Welcome, home, honey. I missed you. Here's your newborn baby. Hop in the car. We've got exactly fourteen minutes to get the older one to the orthodontist before we miss her appointment and have to wait two months to get another."

That, in addition to a couple of kisses hot enough to smoke weeds, was the grand welcome my husband got the last time he came home from deployment. Woo. Hoo.

After months apart, my husband and I sat down next to each other for the first time in the orthodontist's waiting room. While other people's kids walked back and forth from the restroom with their tooth-brushes, Brad held his fussy baby. Our second grader climbed him like a jungle gym. The receptionist asked us how long he'd been home. We looked at our watches and said, in unison, "twenty-seven minutes."

It was as bizarre as it sounds. Almost as bizarre as the first time a stranger asks how long you've been married and you say, "three days." Because some part of you—and some part of that stranger—knows that the first days of marriage and the first days of Homecoming are some-thing special. Something to be marked with reverence, with the donning of new clothes, the killing of the fatted calf, or (if local car retailers have their way) the purchase of a new 4 × 4 diesel truck. Red, I think.

For most military couples, the everyday relentlessness of life does not figure into our Homecoming fantasies. We picture far enough ahead to imagine a sunny day. A pier devoid of other people. A ship that moves swiftly through the water. The instant spotting of our beloved. The envelopment. Sometimes, we can picture him actually in the house or eating at the table. But that is about it.

We tell each other in that last call or e-mail that it will be so good to just have him home and that nothing else matters once we can kiss each other again. He promises he'll fix the disposal, first thing. That he will take care of the poison ivy in the azaleas. That he'll be able to pick up the kids from baseball, really. Well, once he has that 4 × 4 in the driveway. Blue, maybe. He likes blue.

The military knows this Instant Reentry is all fantasy, cut from whole cloth. They try to introduce an element of reality with minions from the Fleet and Family Service Center who want to talk about control of the checkbook, and guys from the highway patrol who want to talk about designated drivers.

But no matter how hard they try, no matter how soon they put the command on stand-down, they can't put the rest of our lives on stand-down. They can't write excuse slips so everyone can stay home from school and from work. They can't stop the car from running out of gas. They can't stop the baseball schedule. They can't keep field day from coming.

In some part of ourselves, we reuniting couples know we need nothing more than to sit alone together. To get used to each other's faces. To become familiar again with the way he stands in a room with his arms folded. The way she never wipes the countertops. The way the baby always cries the instant you get to sleep. We are never prepared for how tired that sailor is. We're never ready for the first time he is annoyed. We never plan on sharing him with his parents and our parents and the neighbors and the disposal and the poison ivy and the kids and the postman and the Army and the Air Force and the dog. The *dog!*

Life has a way of not stopping—not even for Homecoming. Not even for reentry. Yet, somehow, without our close attention, our husbands are reabsorbed. My life and his life become our life together. This is a big piece of what marriage is about. The everyday, the normal, the annoying, the passing of time. This is what we long to share with each other every day that he is gone.

My husband had been home a week before we actually found ourselves alone and uninterrupted. The neighborhood was cast in a post-school-bus silence. We sat in a sunny patch on the carpet in the baby's room. Brad held little Peter while he slept. For hours we talked deeply about . . . nothing. "This is really how I wanted it to be," Brad told me. "Just you and just me."

After Homecoming

Other communities mark the beginning of summer by the clematis climbing up the mailbox. In the military town where I live, we're blessed with one of the most joyful signs of summer of all—the return of the battle group.

Families who haven't had their sailors or Marines around all winter shuffle off their bulky deployment status to bask in the fact that they are at last together again. Even watching from across the street is enough to make you run out and buy a jump rope, or something.

At our kids' baseball game one June night, one family was sporting its newly returned sailor like a two-seater convertible. As he sat on the bleachers with his wife and daughter, all of the team parents leaned forward to meet him.

"Feel like we know you already," one mom told him, patting his shoulder.

"Wife talks about you all the time," said her husband.

"Glad to have you back," said a third, reaching out to shake his hand.

The sailor smiled pleasantly, the way you do when you are the only new one in a group. A dozen half-familiar names scattered past him as we quizzed him about the deployment and wasn't-he-glad-to-be-home and isn't-your-boy-having-a-great-year?

Then we paused, not knowing what else to say—the way kids do when they talk to an exchange student and realize they've used up all their vocabulary words from Spanish 101. The conversation shuffled off to a question about someone he didn't know. His smile faded a little. At the discussion of how the playoffs would be seeded the sailor nodded, then leaned forward to watch the infield practice. He excused himself from listening to the newest antics of someone's crazy neighbor.

I watched him step down the bleachers, speak to his wife, then take a seat in a less-crowded section. The parents there also nodded and smiled to him. But a few minutes later, he walked to his car, brought back a lawn chair and set it up behind the third base line.

"Better view of the plate," he told his daughter.

Better view of the plate? Maybe. Or maybe we have all just forgotten how hard it is for these guys to come home—no matter how much they look forward to it.

Even though this dad had received blow-by-blow accounts of the games and bugged his wife for pictures and called his son on the phone to remind him to keep his bat up, he had still missed the season. Other parents had stamped their feet to keep warm at the first games. Other parents brought the juice boxes. Other parents watched his kid slide into third.

Sometimes, from across the street we wonder how these servicemen and servicewomen can do it. How can they make their legs walk out of the house and down the steps and onto a ship or a plane or a sub that will take them away for months at a time. How can they do it without falling down with grief?

Someone once told me that when men deploy, they don't let themselves think of all they are missing at home. The family becomes like the wiry little figures in a dollhouse—where they leave us, there we stay. No matter how many e-mails or phone calls or pictures they get, they are still surprised to come home to dolls that have learned to walk, use the phone, grow whiskers.

It's a defense mechanism that works, but one that means when a sailor comes home from a deployment, it takes him a few weeks to absorb all of the changes. A few weeks realizing exactly what he missed. A few weeks feeling like a stranger in a strange land.

But they deal with that. They have to. Until baseball season ends. And the group that watched twenty games together disperses. And the sailor becomes part of new groups of parents watching summer swim teams, autumn soccer, winter basketball.

But for right now, this sailor on the sidelines behind third base just has to shout, "Keep your eye on the ball!" and "Get that bat up!" and "Good hit, son! Good hit!" And things will get back to normal—as soon as they possibly can.

Oh-No Moments: What You Forgot While He Was Out to Sea

I'm not sure I should be telling you this, but I think there must be a direct correlation between my husband's perfection and the number of nautical miles that stretch between us.

Gone for a day, and I think of him as endowed with remarkable patience, infinite wisdom, and his own driver's license. Gone for a week, and I remember how the engine-trouble light dared not glow whilst his manliness was in port. Send the guy out to sea for a few months, and he is all that, bay-bee—and good-lookin' to boot.

It is only after Homecoming that I remember that he is not, in fact, Adonis straddling the Earth, but a real live human being. Oh. No.

These Oh-No Moments, of course, come standard with the Deluxe Military Life Package. Here are a few moments you can look forward to.

You Forgot How He Smells

Not the Old Spice shaving cream. Not the Irish Spring wafting from the shower. You forgot the way his luggage makes your bedroom smell of lube oil, industrial disinfectant and—sniff, sniff—could that be the tiniest whiff of . . . what? Canned spinach? Think of those three little words: Tide. With. Bleach.

The Comfort of His Toothbrush in the Holder

After having the bedroom and bathroom to yourself for months on end, you'll go in that first day to brush your teeth and find his toothbrush nestled right up next to yours in the holder. Be struck by how that is the most romantic thing you've ever seen in your life. Resist the urge to run out to buy him a new one. You can't catch West Nile from a toothbrush.

He Cannot Find Anything

You may have lived with the guy for ten years, slept with him, made babies with him, used his razor when he wasn't looking. But now that he has come home from deployment, he spends all his time opening and shutting cabinets, closets, and bureau drawers. Where are the paper towels? Do we have any butter? Have you seen that extra package of razors? Oops.

He Still Needs Privacy

What a surprise. After all those months at sea, you would think he had spent enough time apart from you to last him a lifetime. And now he wants to be alone? Why? When the guy makes a move toward the bathroom or bedroom and shuts the door, resist the urge to allow the children to breathe at him through the doorknob to hurry him along.

You Forgot How to Drive

Despite the fact that you haven't had a car accident in your adult life, the moment the husband unit comes home from deployment, he'll insist that you drive with the hazard lights blinking at all times. Leave an empty Diet Coke can just where his imaginary brake pedal should be. Or let him do all the driving.

He Forgot How to Drive

Now that Mr. Look-out-look-out-LOOK-OOOOOUT! has wrestled you out of the driver's seat, he finds he does not know where he is going. After spending months out of the area, he no longer can find his way to Lowes and has forgotten which lane feeds the downtown tunnel. There is a reason the state police send a cop out to the ship to review standard driving procedures with the sailors. Snickering is strictly prohibited.

He Has Not Been Missing Your Honey-Do List

Even though you think that your list of things for him to do around the house shows him how much you missed him, it doesn't. He comes home from deployment exhausted and ready to be on vacation. Take as much initiative as possible before he gets home so that you can all relax together.

He Is Not G. I. Joe

Whenever my brothers would let me borrow a G. I. Joe ("All right, but no kissing."), Joe always had the decency to kiss Barbie good-bye, then go lie quietly under the bed while he was "at war." Barbie changed clothes, went to work, and redecorated the house from the ground up. She had a high old time until Joe came back to kiss her hello. He was a good kisser. How disconcerting it is as an adult to be with the folks that deployed and find that they have all traveled to foreign ports (without me), quaffed beers (without me), planned a war (without me). G. I. Joe had another life going that whole time. Who knew?

Breaking Up Is Hard to Do

Listen for it. Sprinkled throughout the conversation of names you do not know, expect to hear what J. D. said about this. How J. D. cracked them all up over that. Look for J. D.'s mug in all the pictures. When they see each other again, expect your husband and J. D. to act like they broke up. Imagine what Honeycutt's wife thought of all that post–M*A*S*H conversation about Hawkeye Pierce. Makes you glad your girlfriend lives just up the block.

Homecoming Takes More Than Just a Day

You thought you'd bring your bundle of joy home from the ship, show off the welcome home sign taped to the garage door, and collapse in a heap on the couch. Feels like he never left. Isn't it his turn to unload the dishwasher? But coming all the way home takes longer than you think it will, a few weeks at least. And the more change that has occurred while he is gone—moving, childbirth, puberty, graduations, new cars, new jobs—the longer it will take for him to get back into the swing of things. Have patience. And know that the next six months while Adonis is in your arms will simply fly by.

5 Mobile Homemaking

The Fine Art of Packing, Unpacking, Painting, Arranging, Picture Hanging, Ranting, Sobbing, Laughing Hysterically, and Moving and Moving and Moving Again

MAMIE DOUD EISENHOWER WAS HAPPY to move into the White House at last. In thirty-seven years of Army marriage, it was the first place she and Ike had ever lived with a four-year lease. During Ike's career, the couple moved thirty-five times in thirty-seven years. Thirty-five times. That's got to be a record.

According to her granddaughter and biographer, Susan Eisenhower, Mamie always made light of the ordeal. "I've kept house in everything but an igloo," she would quip. And she had. A woman who had never made a bed before her marriage, Mamie kept house in two-room hovels, two-up/two-down houses, and converted barracks at Camp Meade. Mamie followed Ike to duty in the Panama Canal Zone, France, and the Philippines. And that was BAC—Before Air Conditioning.

I admire the woman; what a tough military wife. I do not want to be her when I grow up, though. No one does—even if you do get to sleep in the Lincoln bedroom at the end. No one wants to move thirty-five times. No one wants to move three times. Moving is hard.

Before I married into the military, I was under the impression that moving was strictly a one-day job. You packed the junk from your room into a yellow milk crate and a couple of boxes. The moving men (or your boyfriend of the day) hefted your bed and your dresser onto a truck. You drove to the new place, put the new key in the new door, and ordered a pizza.

Voilà. You moved. Big whoop.

Not anymore. Not if you are a grown woman, are married, and have kids. Not if your possessions fill more than a yellow milk crate. Now a move is a significant life change—like leaving home for the first time, getting divorced, changing careers.

Moving is a Very Big Deal. No matter how many times you do it—even if you do it thirty-five times—every single move is difficult. Senior wives say time and again that you never get used to moving. Dreading a move is not the sign of a weakling. It's the experienced woman's normal reaction to a life-changing event.

Moving isn't the end of the world. You're losing a house, a neighborhood, a grocery store that stocks pine nuts and sun-dried tomatoes—not your marriage and not your family. You, too, are going to become skilled at making the transition, and at recognizing and organizing the changes. Take notes. There will be a test.

Doesn't the Military Move for You?

What's funny about military life is that the people around you expect you to be used to it. This cracks me up, kind of. People will think (and tell you) that anyone who has moved eight times in nine years should be used to it; it should be old hat. They will wonder aloud at your complaints, asking, "Doesn't the military move for you?"

Well, yeah, if you consider moving simply the act of packing boxes, hauling beds to the third floor, and reinstalling the washing machine. But that isn't the hard part. That's the physical part, the list of things to do.

Turns out moving isn't a one-weekend kind of thing. The physical move takes about a month, from beginning of boxes to end of boxes. Experts say you should allow at least six months before you expect to feel really settled in your new home. That's true—sometimes. Other times, you'll look up and find that you really are settled in at the six-month mark. And then there's the lucky dog who settles in at two months. But the older you are, the shier you are, the more times you move, the harder it gets to settle in.

Lately I have begun to think we need to allow at least a year to move, body and soul. Easily. This may be the best way to think about moves in general—that you will pass through its seasons as inexorably as you pass through the seasons of a year. From summer to fall, winter to spring.

I've moved thirteen times in seventeen years. That isn't normal. My husband is in a job that moves more often than most other military people move. It's part of his work. And, yes, he's a very good kisser. That's why I keep going with him. Here are the stories of those seasons of our moves.

Summer: It's Not the Heat, It's the Humidity

A move creeps up on you, just like summer. One day you are running around shivering in your sporty yellow slicker; the next day you wake up realizing not a soul in your house owns a pair of shorts that actually fits. And it's 93 degrees out there.

To my way of thinking, PCS orders ought to come accompanied by fireworks, barbecues, and a big, fat, tax-free check. To pay for all that anxiety-reducing ice cream.

They don't.

Instead, one day your spouse will just mention in conversation that he recently talked to his detailer or monitor. That the available jobs were all bad. That the detailer, that jolly friend who sends you where you do not want to go, is talking about orders to Langley Air Force Base or Wright-Patterson or Malmstrom. Wherever that is.

The conversation is so vague, you won't take it seriously. You can no more imagine yourself moving on this summery day than you can imagine snow in the air or ice on the roads. Weird. This is a huge base. Surely they'll come up with a new job for him right here.

Then, one evening while you're knee-deep in a piña colada and you have forgotten the whole silly idea of a move, the husband unit drops the bomb. He has a fabulous new job. You'll be moving in seventy-eight days. To Offut AFB. In Omaha.

Your mind races. Omaha. Omaha. Where is the country Omaha? On the one hand, you may be secretly happy to get rid of the house with the uncomfortable bathtub. You may be delighted to desert the Yard That Will Not Grow Grass.

On the other hand, you're filled with dread. How are you going to make it through another move? Other moving experts will tell you to clean out your drawers, set up your garage sale, and start tracking down points with your pal, Fannie Mae. I'm not going there. I'm going to tell you how some of us make it through seasons of our moves—and assure you that you'll make it too.

The Power of Positive Thinking Is Not One of My Powers

Some people handle the prospect of a move better than others. I am not one of them. But my girlfriend, Lori, is. She looks at a move so positively, you would think sky-blue glasses were surgically attached to her head.

Even when her husband got orders to a third-world country, Lori looked at the 65 percent literacy rate, the marked rise in Islamic fundamentalism, the landscape like Tatooine during a drought—and couldn't wait to go.

She e-mailed all of us whose Christmas pictures decorate her refrigerator door. "We are very happy and looking forward to our next exotic adventure. We are looking forward to enjoying the beautiful beaches, seeing the Roman ruins, camel rides in the Sahara, and possible visits to the other Mediterranean countries such as France, Italy, Greece, Malta, Spain, and Egypt."

Lori wasn't faking it. She didn't don those synthetic rose-colored glasses that used to be standard issue for military wives. She wasn't spouting Pollyanna-ish drivel that would dissolve in real disaster. She actually went to all those places, did all those things.

Lori is the kind of military spouse who sees her way clear to the good in every move, the beauty in every place. She still chides me for living on base when we were all stationed in Japan. I don't. I was happy to skip the kerosene heaters, tatami floors, no clothes dryer, and Japanese neighbors who preferred absolute quiet. I was, after all, raising The Loud Family. In public.

But Lori and her family lived in the *chō*. Years after she moved away, Lori still remembered the tinny music from the broom salesman's truck, the cheerful *ohayō gozaimasu* in her living room from an unexpected neighbor dropping by, the temple gong at dawn calling monks to prayer. I love her for that.

By rights, Lori's eyes should be the most brilliant shade of cerulean blue. For she sees what I long to see in every move—the chance to do something different, to see what she can see.

Whenever we are due for orders, I go out and get a pair of sky-blue sunglasses to stash in the car. They are the signal to me that I'm in training. The more I wear the glasses, the more my mind believes the day is brighter and better than it is—even though it is a shock when I take them off.

It also helps to surround myself with friends like Lori—the kind that have character in just the places I don't. She filters the perils in life so that they fade next to the possibilities; I panic first, find a solution later, and slug through the thing last of all.

We get to the same place, Lori and me. But I'm plodding, flat-footed, eyes fixed on sand. And Lori rides perched on the camel, wrapped in a mantel of bluest sky.

Moving Is Not *My* Idea, So Why Is Everyone Mad at Me?

"I dread telling you this," announced a longtime friend who lives in my neighborhood, "but . . . we're moving."

"No kidding," I said, expecting to hear that Civilian Ellen's husband had been promoted to Chicago or L.A., or something profitable like that. "Where are you headed?"

She put her hand over her mouth. Muttered the name of a neighborhood less than fifteen minutes away. "We're going to have to change schools," she confessed.

"This year?"

"No," she said guiltily, squeezing her shoulders into her clavicle, as though I were likely to whack her with my diaper bag. "I'll drive the kids back and forth for the rest of the school year. We'll go to the same pool this summer, I promise! It's not like I'm going to give up any of my old haunts or anything."

I still didn't get the fear factor at work here. "What are you not telling me?"

"Nothing else. It's just that I've already told a couple of people from the neighborhood and they got mad," she said. "Really mad. At me."

Now I was smelling the packing tape. No wonder the neighbors were mad. Ol' Ellen had made the mistake of being absolutely indispensable to the neighborhood. She was known for catching stray kids and feeding them a healthy snack if their moms didn't get to the bus stop on time. She checked on the elderly during snowstorms. She volunteered to teach Sunday school, remembered the chips for the soccer team, made the only edible potato salad at block parties. Realtors listed "Ellen" before "Location" amongst the assets of the neighborhood.

And now she was moving? Outrageous.

"I don't know how you military people do it," Civilian Ellen said. "You moved, what? A million times? And nobody gets mad at you."

"Sure, but I'm a professional," I said smugly. "You think this comes easy? It's an act of sheer will to make people hope that you'll move soon. We've had to teach the kids to sell candy door-to-door. We set alarms so we can rotate cars at all hours until the neighbors think we're running a crack house. Even the dog helps out. He opens the screen door and lets himself out every time he hears a gas grill ignite. It's exhausting."

"Geez, I wish I had thought ahead like you," Ellen said. "We never intended to live in this house forever, but I didn't think moving would make people mad. We're forty. How old do we have to be before we own our own garage?"

I hooked my thumbs through my belt loops. "You just don't understand. Even if you have an ironclad reason to move, like PCS orders, buying a house in another neighborhood sends a clear signal. It says that having a two-car garage and a lawn big enough for a football game is far more important than having the honor and privilege of seeing your neighbor unload her grocery bags for the rest of her life. By putting the sign on the lawn, you've made the school substandard, the street congested, and their house in need of a coat of paint."

Ellen cried, "And I just wanted a place to put my garden hose."

Disentangling from the Neighborhood

I had to take pity on Civilian Ellen. What she really needed was a disentangler. That's what I need every time I move. What is a disentangler? In Japan, when people want a divorce without embarrassment, conflict, or confrontation, they hire a firm of "couple-busters," or disentanglers. These guys don't just set out to catch your spouse in an affair; they lure him into one. The firm sends out a pretty young thing to go and start an affair, get evidence, and then disappear.

It's all very polite. And it's exactly what I need to extract myself from the neighborhood and the school system without hurting anyone's feelings.

Here's how it should work: I would invite this stellar, organized, not-so-good-lookin' disentangler to a neighborhood party. She would bring a little something to share that she'd learned to cook from her brother, Emeril. Then she would tell everyone how she loved having crowds of kids at her house for hours at a time. She'd zip around in a fifteen-passenger van and offer to run the baseball players to all their practices. Which is usually my job.

Once the neighbors were hooked on the disentangler, she'd deliver the kicker. She would volunteer to teach Sunday school and organize the Christmas pageant single-handedly. At the moment the neighbors took her up on it, I'd give them my most hurt look and simply disappear.

I am as clever as clever. I know, you don't have to tell me.

Unfortunately, there are no disentanglers in this country (but what a great franchise). When we military spouses pull out of our neighborhoods, we have to expect some hurt feelings among the people we are leaving behind. People who are sad or hurt or angry to see you go are much, much better friends than people who ask, "How many more days before you leave?"

It goes both ways. Give your old friends a little time to get used to a new move. They'll come round.

Sweating Out Short Timer's Disease

When my husband came upstairs to check on my progress, I cast myself across my bed and pretended to read the last six chapters of my book club book. Which was meeting in half an hour. "I'm not so sure I'm going to book club," I told him.

"Because . . ."

"Because maybe I'm catching a cold," I said with a sniffle. "My throat is a little scratchy." I pulled the covers higher around my shoulders and tried to look as pathetic as possible.

He wasn't buying it.

"You ought to go," Brad cajoled. "You said you would go, so you really ought to go."

Easy for him to say. Because Brad never gets Short Timer's Disease. Even though this would be move number nine, Brad still is the kind of person who likes to end things as completely as possible, tying up each area of his life with neat brown paper and some good strong twine. His ideal is to work so consistently up to the very end that people exclaim, "You're leaving already?! I had no idea!"

But he's weird that way.

I guess the more common variety of Short Timer's Disease afflicts people about four months before their departure. They can't go to the PTA because they're moving. They can't get that project done because they're moving. They can't donate to the new playground because (you guessed it) they're moving. Their lives in this location crawl inexorably to a complete stop, until you have to wonder if respiration itself is beyond them.

My version of a good ending is one that takes even me completely by surprise. I think the military should never tell me about anything in advance, especially not a move. I should just go about my business, living my life and eating ice cream until one day the moving truck shows up like the Grim Reaper. Granted, it might be an unpleasant surprise, but at least I wouldn't have to clean that chimichanga off the microwave.

Once we have orders, I can't help wishing we were already gone. I wish we would never have to face tunnel traffic on Friday afternoon, never have to chase the dog away from Squirrel City, never again hit every traffic light on Arlington Boulevard. When it's time to go, I just want to go.

But that isn't what happens. Instead, my son Sam came in and dived onto the bed next to me, the sharp points of his cowboy boots digging into my hip. "Daddy said to kiss you good-bye, Mommy," he said, hesitating a moment, then dropping a kiss on my knee. "Good-bye."

So I dutifully got up, found my shoes, and put on a little lipstick. I couldn't skip through the last chapters of the move. Brad was right. This wasn't just a novel I was skimming. It was the book of my life. I can't leave sloppy—or worse—empty pages by failing to complete the assigned work. That would destroy all feeling for the character. Especially when the character we're talking about is me.

Geographic Bachelor: Take Me with You!

Don't urge me to leave you or turn back from you. Where you go I will go, and where you stay I will stay.
—Ruth 1:16

Remember that time you called me in the middle of the night from the Arabian Sea? It was so late I had to drag myself from sleep to answer the phone. I don't know if I told you this, but the moment I heard the hesitation in the overseas line, my stomach plunged. I felt the sting of adrenaline in the crooks of my elbows, on the backs of my knees. I thought you were about to tell me that someone died. Or that you'd been fired. Or that the deployment had been extended until the end of time.

Instead, you were calling because you had to tell me right away that you might be getting different orders from the ones you expected. Nothing definite, mind you. But the detailer had called to talk to you about taking orders to Washington, D.C.

"Tell me again what you're upset about," I asked, wondering if I had heard all you said. "Is it a bad job?"

"No, no, it's a good job," you answered. "But it's in D.C. You hate D.C. You said you'd never live there again. And I just want to know. Will you come with me?"

I fell back against the pillows. Shut my eyes. You thought you were asking if I would pack up the stuff for the twelfth time in our fifteen years of marriage and move for a year to a city that pleases other people but fails to please me. But you were asking more than that. From across the world I could hear you wondering whether it was

continued on page 112

**Geographic Bachelor:
Take Me with You!** *continued*

worth it. Whether living with you was worth it.

After all, plenty of people go the geographic bachelor route when confronted with orders to D.C. for a year or two. They see their families on the weekends when they can get away. Sometimes they make it out of the office early on a Friday afternoon. Sometimes they stay home Sunday night until the children are fast asleep, and then drive through I-95 weekend traffic late into the night.

We can't do that. I'd worry about you. Just the same way I'd worry about you squatting in an apartment with four other guys, eating out of fast-food bags and microwave boxes, working too late, running on empty. Our friends say geographic bachelorhood was more expensive than they thought it would be. People at parties confide that it is misery, even if your marriage is solid and you have a very, very good reason to do it—like a senior in high school, a special-needs child, a six-month tour.

I don't want that for you or for me. But moving? I don't want to move. I want our daughter to play basketball for Coach Steve next year. I want to stay in this town, where I fit as though I were born here. I want my paint to stay on the walls, my curtains on the rods.

My civilian friends think that moving for such a short amount of time is insane. They think it is outlandish for you to even ask, the height of selfishness to move a seventh grader, a third grader, a baby.

But they don't know what it is like to live apart from you for seven months, much less a year. When you called from the ship about

Autumn: A Season of Fresh Beginnings

Starting the New Year in January is absolutely archaic. God rest ye merry gentlemen, the year does not start in January. In America, the new year starts fresh and sparkly with new notebooks and blue jeans—in September. In most places, even the fiscal year starts in October. Autumn is the sign of the bright and shiny new year.

It is also the sign of the bright and shiny new move. In the autumn season of a move, you actually stop getting ready to move and just do it. The packers come. You turn off the phone, forward the mail, scrub behind the fridge. You paint the new place. Toss a bottle of White Zin in the fridge and your move is just about done—except for the emotional upheaval. Such fun.

The Glorious Opportunities of Moving

Despite the fact our house-to-be strongly resembled a walk-in closet equipped with hot plate, no one in this family actually wanted to move. Go figure.

My husband moaned about leaving his current favorite-job-of-all-time. Our son refused to relinquish his neighborhood roaming plan. Our daughter wood-puttied herself into her room. And baby Pete howled at the very thought of trying to sleep without the comforting rumble of jet noise.

It was the outside of enough, however, when Jimmery Quinn, my daughter's beloved dwarf hamster, up and *died* the week before our move. Poor little fella. The dog must have squealed about the move to D.C. and young Jimmery couldn't face the horror.

Can't really blame him.

But I'm the mom. During a move it is my job, yea, my God-given responsibility, to make this Trail of Tears seem like a walk through the Valley of the Shadow of Opportunity! I must make myself as cheery and chipper as . . . as . . . as a hamster! Not the kind of hamster that (hopefully) lies undisturbed beneath the hydrangea bush, but an upbeat hamster just the same.

So what glorious opportunities and lessons do I sell my family in the weeks before the move?

Opportunity to contemplate material goods. There's nothing like touching every item you own to convince yourself that you don't need to own so many items. I mean, what is the wisdom of owning four sets of china when you must *unpack* four sets of china—in aforementioned walk-in closet? Zen military family sleeping on futons in a bare room sounds like Swiffer Heaven right about now, believe you me.

Opportunity to shift identities. Here's one for the kiddies: Nothing like a move to promote the changing of one's name, interests, appearance, and personal flaws under the philosophy of This Time I'll Be Different. I'm promoting shifts like Kelsey's plan to

these orders, I knew what I was missing. Now that you are home from deployment, I'm even more certain of what I cannot live without.

Take me with you, not because I have to come, not because we can't afford to live apart. Take me with you because you are more to me than an extra set of hands to unload the dishwasher, carry the car seat, paint the bathroom.

Take me with you because my happiness is hearing your car putter into the driveway. My joy is the look we exchange when our kids are so funny, we dare not laugh out loud. My pleasure in life is the knowledge that if I fall asleep reading, you will reach over and turn off the light, set my book on the floor, check that the baby monitor is turned on.

I once read a letter to Dear Abby from an elderly widower. He said that his wife would call him at work sometimes, even when they were young, and ask him to come home early for no particular reason. He never did. And now that she was dead, the man wrote to tell Abby that he finally understood just what she had been asking.

I don't want to move. But, more importantly, I don't want you to know what it's like to live in a house without me. I don't want to miss any of our time together for any reason—other than the good of the Navy. I don't want us to have regrets about the way we lived our lives.

Boxes can be unpacked. Curtains can be resewn. Children can be pushed up the steep learning curve at a new school. Let's move. Because where you are is always home to me.

Get Rid of the Boxes

One of the best ways to feel organized quickly is to get rid of the boxes. Tell yourself you will be through every single box in two weeks. Don't put boxes in the attic or basement. Don't shove them out in the garage or cover them with a tablecloth and pretend they're an extra countertop. Get rid of the boxes. Resolve to only open one box at a time and completely empty one box before you start another.

change her name to "KellSeee" or the alphabetically challenging "Qelsie." Sam campaigns for metal studs that will make him appear to have small silver fangs thrust through his lower lip. I plan to feign an affinity for emptying cereal bowls before dinner time.

Opportunity to enlighten young friends. A move to our nation's capital seems pretty glamorous to thems that never moved. Neighborhood children encircle our house to witness the enviable summer drama playing itself out before their eyes—the parties, the packing, the twitching Mommy eyelid that means Trouble For Sam. Ka-pow! How lucky can one family be?

Opportunity to plumb new depths. Opportunity knocks not just for the juvenile set. I've found that anxiety over where to put a six-foot china cabinet in a house with no unbroken six-foot stretch of wall has visibly deepened the crevice between my brows. Geez, I can just about hide a lipstick in there. So handy when storage space is at a premium.

Opportunity to divest. What is it about our refrigerator that breeds an assortment of jams, jellies, sauces, dressings, mustards, curries, custards, and buttermilk (?) so vast the door itself has developed a gut? Crazy Landlord insists I throw this stuff out *and* clean behind the refrigerator—like I've never done either before. Huh. Somebody up there must know me.

Opportunity to commune with nature. Sharing counter space with a superhighway of ants. Scraping spider webs so strong they apparently hold the house on its foundation. These are things that make me appreciate moving away. Nothing brings more joy, though, than closing the salad bar of pansies, tulip bulbs, and impatiens our yard squirrels have been munching for years. Let 'em starve.

Opportunity to ponder beauty. Now that my walls are painted shades of jaunty yellow, frisky blue, and crisp apple green, Crazy Landlord insists we return our house to its original ugliness. His shade, Berkshire White, is the same color as a three-day-dead cadaver. What a world.

Opportunity to terrify small children. Just when the kids think it's safe to seek succor from Mommy, I get to pull out my creepy *The Others* impression. Children clutched to my bosom, I whisper, "No one can make us leave this house. This is our house. This is our house. This is our house." You thought Nicole Kidman was scary.

Indulging in all of these opportunities wears me—and every other moving mother—quite to a frazzle. Move over Jimmery. Somehow the peaceful shade beneath the hydrangea is looking mighty good to me.

Feed the Movers?

Everyone has an opinion about whether or not you should feed the movers. If you feed them, are they less likely to steal from you? If you don't feed them, will they understand that you had quite enough to deal with and pay for already that day?

I don't know. I'm that kind of wacky broad who can't have people in her house without offering them something to drink. I usually skip the morning donuts. No one eats them but me. I try to have Cokes and water in the cooler and invite them to help themselves all day long. Shoot, anyone who is unloading the contents of my bathroom cupboard has got to be family.

I usually provide lunch, but I don't get all fancy. The last group of movers we hired informed me that their previous customer *roasted a turkey* for them after they informed her they were sick of pizza. In the oven she spent three days cleaning? I don't think so.

These guys do deserve some nourishment, though. Some of them, notably the packers, are professionals. I appreciate the job they do. And some of them are day laborers. Moving ain't no picnic. It's a job your own brothers won't offer to undertake for you. The movers earn every dime they make—one dime at a time. I appreciate the brawn and the back brace. Have a sandwich.

House Envy: Is Anyone Ever Satisfied?

House Envy has gotten to be something of a chronic condition with me. I have moved so many times that even when I am not house hunting, I am sifting through available properties.

Top Ten Things (besides Pizza) to Give the Movers

According to a recent survey by the Illinois Movers Association, movers don't think we householders are obligated to feed them. However, they do appreciate anything we are able to provide. Here's my list of the most important things to provide your movers.

1. *Drinks.* Set them up in a neutral location, such as a cooler on the porch, patio, or driveway. Water—either bottled or in disposable cups—is the drink of choice followed by Gatorade, Classic Coke, or Mountain Dew. Never give movers alcoholic beverages.

2. *A designated bathroom.* Point out at the beginning of the day the bathroom you'd prefer the movers to use. It's less embarrassing for all concerned.

3. *Time.* Contrary to popular belief, movers are not dragging their feet, hoping that this job will last forever. A quick-lunch solution means they'll be gone that much faster.

4. *Choice.* If you plan to bring in fast food, tell the movers which restaurants are nearby and ask which one they'd prefer. They'll appreciate being consulted.

5. *Subs.*

6. *Chicken.*

7. *Barbecue sandwiches.*

8. *Burgers.*

9. *Burritos.*

10. *Cold cuts, cheese, bread, condiments.* Many movers mentioned this option. It also helps get rid of nine jars of mustard.

It's my own private psoriasis. I can usually control it by following a strict Pottery Barn–free diet and coaching myself to remember that Someday My House Will Come.

But House Envy does flair up. It happened most recently when my book club hostess settled next to me to pick my brain about her upcoming move to Europe. It was not an ideal moment. For, while she was discussing Realtors, I was mentally rearranging *my* furniture in *her* house. So rude, I know. Like imagining yourself kissing your hostess's husband. Passionately. Which I would never do.

Susan's restored Victorian needed no mental redecoration. It was bedecked in antique sideboards and Persian carpets and large-scale art. Its perfection, however, was not stopping me from wildly painting my own cheery colors on her walls. Placing my books in her cabinets. Ripping down valances with my bare hands and installing lovely blue-and-white drapes lined with yellow something.

I froze. Susan was looking at me funny. "Did you just say something?" I asked.

"I said I was sad about selling this house," Susan said.

"Anyone would be," I replied, reaching out to pat her knee while simultaneously calculating the asking price. I might be able to afford it if I sold everything I owned, brainwashed a dozen college students into channeling me their parents' money, and sent parents and students alike out in the street in saffron robes to collect alms.

"I look around this house and everyone says that it is beautiful," Susan paused. "But in the three years I owned it I've done nothing but fight with this house. It doesn't work for me. It never has."

Fight with a house? A house as perfect as this one? In thirteen moves, I've had plenty of houses to knock out and slap down. I've had ugly houses with wall-to-wall carcinogens. I've had houses built to withstand hurricanes in true military cinder block style. I've had houses so dark they rival the Black Hole of Calcutta.

How could this beautiful house be wrong for anyone? This is the kind of house featured in magazines with dentil molding and tongue-in-groove everything, rewired and replumbed to twenty-first century standards. How could it be wrong?

"There is nowhere we can sit and eat," Susan said, looking around at the formal rooms. "None of us come down here. We watch TV all crammed together in a little room upstairs. My stuff doesn't even fit here right. The rooms are too long and narrow and the windows are in all the wrong places."

I could see what she meant, then. Susan had gotten to the place where her house was not her friend, not her champion. It was simply wrong. Realtors forget to tell you that part when you are looking for a house.

When we move into a new house, we are full of hopes for what we will do with it, how we will live, who we will be. Sometimes, though, the fit of the house, like the fit of a shoe, is just wrong. Sometimes a house can feel like it hates you, like it wishes you would move. It can be

Location, Location, Location

Certain military jobs are notorious for their long hours. At one point during your spouse's career, he'll have one of those jobs. Do yourself a favor and live close to the base during those tours. Your husband's shorter commute may bring him home for dinner from time to time, and it keeps a tired driver off the road. Something to think about.

The Kids

The autumn season of the move, with all its endings and new beginnings, is the part of moving that gets to kids the most. See chapter 6 for more ideas about getting your children through a move.

a living, breathing opponent who refuses to conform, who will not get along, who is stingy with hot water until you could cry from its cruelty and shudder at its indifference.

I've had those houses. Houses that make you shake the dust from your feet and the address from your memory. For our houses are meant to be allies, not enemies. Sometimes even the most modest house can wrap itself around the way we live. It's got just the right number of steps from front door to kitchen. Groceries seem to put themselves away and the dog has a place to light undisturbed. Keys can always be found and the front lamp glows a welcome, even when you thought you forgot to turn it on.

That is the house that you wrap around you like a quilt, a coat, a bathrobe. The house you soak in until you feel better. The house you cannot bear to leave. And when you have moved away from that house, moved away from any number of those houses, be prepared for the most virulent outbreak of House Envy.

Melding into the Neighborhood

I collect moving tips from the "Neighbors" page of *Better Homes and Gardens* magazine. I know that sooner or later I will have a use for them. Sigh.

When I clipped out an article about making a neighborhood map, it seemed a grand plan. I could just picture the kids and me moseying up and down our new street, meeting the neighbors, exchanging phone numbers, and writing down the names of all our new friends on our little homemade map to hang on the fridge. I mean, how cute is that?

Instead, I sat on the front stoop of my new house in D.C., waiting for a moving van that was four hours late. Up and down the quiet street, houses drew into themselves under a muggy sky. Who was I kidding? I'd never do it. I'd never have the nerve to knock on people's doors. All hail Mrs. Dork and her dorkful children with map and markers and awkward manners in tow!

Never gonna happen.

The one neighbor we had managed to meet during the house-hunting trip hoped we didn't have a dog (we do), hoped we were aware that no kids live around here (we weren't), hoped we wouldn't move out too soon (we will). And I had already forgotten her name.

As the moving van lumbered up the hill, I shook myself a little. This looked like a street where we would lock our cars in the driveway, avert our eyes while mowing the lawn, live inside the confines of our own front door. Some neighborhoods are like that.

By dinner time, the movers had tossed empty mattress boxes on the lawn, leaned against the truck, and watched dumbfounded as a little widow lady in a blue linen dress with matching handbag toddled back up the street.

After a respectful silence, the driver asked, "Have you lived in this neighborhood before?"

"No," I answered, looking down at the rose-embossed card in my hand. Mrs. Rapp had scrawled her phone number across the back, in case I needed to know where to find anything locally.

"Then you don't know any of the people that came by here?" he said. "Not those moms with the strollers? Not the lady in the green van? Not that guy with the Volvo or the one on the bike?"

"That was the same guy," the other mover told him. "He just waved from the bike."

"And you forgot the kids with the party invitation," the third guy added. "You don't know any of those people?"

"No." I said. "I guess they were just . . . introducing themselves?"

"Man, I've never seen such a friendly neighborhood," said the driver heading back inside the truck.

"They ain't like this in the projects," the other guy added.

They ain't like this anywhere. By the time the moving van pulled away, no fewer than a dozen people had stopped by to say hello. Five different neighbors had invited us to the annual block party the next day. My landlady had dropped off a dozen chocolate-chip cookies on a paper plate.

The movers and I looked upon these events as though we were shepherds in a field surrounded by great portents of wonder and joy. But what was the big deal? Sure, the people who lived on this street stopped by for thirty seconds to shake my hand and tell me their names. That's some kind of crazy miracle?

It is according to the movers—and me.

How many times have I seen a house stand empty in my neighborhood? How many times have I looked askance at a scraggly yard and hoped for new tenants? How many times have I seen a moving van pull up and then pretended I didn't see the newcomers because I didn't have any lipstick on or I was in a hurry or I felt guilty for not making them a lasagna?

Mrs. Rapp and her neighbors humbled me.

So I've got a better idea for the "Neighbors" page of *Better Homes and Gardens*. It doesn't involve children, markers, or homemade maps. It's just this: When you see a moving van in front of a house, consider it an invitation. On that one golden day, there is no pressure to clean your house, offer refreshments, or even be in the mood to meet new neighbors. The first time you see a neighbor, consider it an invitation to freely offer your name, your hand, your welcome without any suspicion, any awkwardness. Otherwise, Mrs. Dork and her dorkful children may be knocking on the doors of every house on your block. Someone's gotta do it.

Christmas: Think She's Gonna Make It After All

I would have liked to blame my optimism on all those little Christmas lights twinkling in every storefront or on my children, who were actually singing carols throughout the mall. I would have liked to blame it on the effects of Move Number Nine.

Since it all took place during the season of naughty and nice, however, the blame for my uncharacteristic optimism must have rested at the feet of the bronzed demigod lounging with the other stylists in the front of the hair salon. The sight of his muscles bulging beneath a black T-shirt, the crisp black hair dipping artfully across his forehead, reminded me that my own hair had reached critical mass.

"Honeys," I said to the children. "Do you two think you could wait long enough for Mommy to get a haircut?"

I knew haircuts and children weren't usually a good combination, but Brad wouldn't be home from his trip until Friday at the earliest, and I desperately needed to do something with my hair.

"Can we play with everything in your purse?" five-year-old Sam asked. "Even the gum?"

"Sure," I answered recklessly.

"Let's go!" Kelsey said, making a beeline back to the salon. I followed them, suddenly doubtful at the thought of another impetuous relationship with a hairdresser.

"Why do I do this?" I wondered as I followed the children. I don't have good hair. Other people have good hair—long beautiful tresses that grow. My hair doesn't grow—it crawls, creeps, oozes down my head like a cap of cold spaghetti. Finding someone who can figure out what to do with it calls for three wise men and a star pointing directly over the salon.

After moving to northern Virginia months before, I had easily found a pediatric dentist, an affordable veterinarian, the Talbots outlet. But I still hadn't unearthed a soul to cut my hair. Inflict a haircut upon me, yes. Six different hairdressers had managed that. But a good haircut? Impossible.

"Are you taking walk-ins?" I asked El Gorgeouso casually, trying not to appear like the kind of woman who makes life-altering decisions lightly. The kids grabbed the nearest bench and started excavating for gum, crayons, and a couple of stray army guys.

"Why, yes," he said, coming lazily to his feet. He looked like one of those miracle men who appear on Oprah and transform plain women into sirens. I had visions.

Then El Gorgeouso walked me to the front desk and delivered me into the hands of his younger brother, Khalil. Lovely, but wouldn't he rather be wearing a black T-shirt?

I followed Khalil back to his chair, silently cursing the Powers That Be. Hanging out at the Pentagon with their identical haircuts administered in their identical barbershops right where they work, they couldn't possibly understand the many hazards of moving. If they did, they wouldn't send one-third of our population PCS orders every year. If they did, they would be able to explain why this move—our ninth in eleven years—was taking so long to feel like home?

The stylist sat down next to me while I described the ooblek on my head. "Don't follow the style that's there," I warned him. "My last stylist was having an affair with some married guy, so no two bits of my hair are alike."

Khalil combed through my hair silently, pulled it this way and that. Mused over it, brooded.

"You know," he said thoughtfully, "your hair is hard to cut. It's so straight and has that tendency to stand out. See, I think it is a little short on top—we could have more length here. A better shape."

Hope blossomed in my bitter little soul. Could this be that moment in the move—just like that moment during the holidays—when you finally stop feeling overwhelmed? That moment when you turn the lights on the tree, when you believe none of the members of the Christmas pageant will be wearing "I'm an Angel" T-shirts, when you're convinced the kids won't be opening bags of flour on Christmas morning? Could this be the moment of the move when I would actually feel *moved*?

Khalil washed. Cut. Blow-dried. Applied goo. Turned me to the mirror.

Sweet mystery of life, at last I've found you!

"Mommy, Mommy!" The kids ran toward me as I left the chair. "Mommy, you're so beautiful!"

I paid the bill and passed El Gorgeouso, still lounging in the window.

"We better get crackin,'" Sam said around a mouthful of gum. "Next stop?"

"Home," I said happily. "Let's go home."

Winter: Why Don't I Feel Settled Yet?

Even after you have passed the Christmas moment in your move when you believe you actually have settled in, you may reach a long, empty cold spell. Everyone has stopped asking you if you feel at home because you've lied and lied and lied about how everything is just fine. Good for you. People like to hear that a move is No Big Deal.

But the truth is, you may have the kids in twelve sports apiece, but you don't know anyone. You've met plenty of people, but you don't *know* anyone. You don't have a real buddy to meet for coffee. You can't think of an alternate spot to attend Midnight Mass on Christmas Eve. You realize that you couldn't find a store that sells Rit dye for the Girl Scout craft project unless you went back to your last duty station. It is the Winter of Your Discontent. And, although you don't feel good, these blahs are a very good sign. They are the signal that you are breaking away from your old life. Grieving the loss. Getting ready to move into your new life.

Warding Off the Black Dog

I am in the kitchen. I spoon rice cereal and peaches into the baby who is sitting in the high chair. Pop Silver Queen corn into boiling water. Cast a blue-and-white-checked cloth over the table. Hand a beer to my husband. Brush the nap of my passing son's flattop as if I were trailing my palm across a display of holiday velvets. He smiles. I am in my element, all things to all people. For the first time in a month, the Black Dog is nowhere in sight. A blessed, if temporary, relief. Because the Black Dog that plagues me isn't a member of this family, but the depression that arrives with the cardboard boxes every time we move—including Move Number Twelve.

Ugh. The Black Dog. I lifted the term from Winston Churchill, who aptly described his depressive episodes that way. According to his biographer, William Manchester, Churchill was often overwhelmed by feelings of hopelessness in times of disappointment, rejection, or bereavement. Churchill's episodes were bad enough that he didn't like to sleep near a balcony or stand too close to the edge of a train platform or the side of a ship.

I'm not that bad. But many of us are. Depression is the most common psychological problem in the United States, a problem that the average American, with his complex lifestyle, is ten times more likely to experience than his 1950s counterpart.

Dealing with Depression during a Move

According to the American Psychological Association, more than 19 million Americans suffer from depression yearly, and women are twice as likely as men to experience a major depressive episode. Although there isn't a magic trick to cure depression, experts believe that episodes can be prevented when you learn to anticipate risk factors. Moving definitely qualifies as a risk factor.

Dr. Michael J. Yapko, clinical psychologist and author of five books on depression, says that much of what causes depression can be unlearned. The following tips about avoiding depression during a move are based on Dr. Yapko's work.

1. *Stay focused.* Moving is a part of military life. It is often a stepping-stone to a better job, a promotion, a secure retirement. Part of attaining those goals is sacrificing the stability that homeownership provides. When you catch yourself longing for the fantasy—*stop.* Remind yourself that every choice in life precludes another choice. Rental houses and base housing are a part of paying your dues.

2. *Align expectations with reality.* One of the things we learn from our society is to apply the standards of "it's gotta be fast" and "it's gotta be easy" to everything—even when it is unrealistic and potentially damaging. By expecting to make lifelong friends in two weeks and expecting the family to be instantly and easily settled, we set ourselves up for

For me, and for many military spouses, depression is an element of every move. The dog doesn't visit too often during the deployment, and he's nowhere to be seen on my birthday, but something about missing my girlfriends and not knowing where to buy shin guards and talking to a dry cleaner who does not know my name causes the Black Dog to come forth and take up a prominent position at my side. And he stinks.

His favorite trick is to lead me down a little path of erroneous thought. He'll start with one normal idea and look over his shoulder to see if I'm coming. Then he'll lead a little further on, until I'm sobbing over man's inhumanity to man and he is frolicking in his favorite puddle of misery.

The other day, his path started when he innocently pointed out an old woman in a yellow T-shirt crossing the street in front of our car.

"What a pretty color," he suggested.

"I've got a shirt that color," I agreed.

"My heavens that woman has a bent back. Probably didn't drink enough milk in her youth."

"I don't drink enough milk," I muttered.

"Hmm, that's true. You'll probably look just like her when you are old. Bent over. Maybe even bent double." Black Dog paused, tongue lolling with glee, waiting for me to picture my own bent back in a yellow T-shirt. Then he delivers the clincher.

"So sad. You'll wear your yellow T-shirt. You'll be old. Your life will be over. And then you'll die."

Shoulda seen it coming. Pretty much every path the Black Dog walks me down ends right there. Which is silly. What am I going to do? Die of old age next Tuesday?

There was a time when I trailed the Black Dog down all his miserable paths, sniffing out "reasons" why my kids have big feet (toxic hormones in the water), why there is a gate in my backyard (so ax murderers can get in), why the neighbor did not call back (busy telling everyone else not to be my friend). I don't go with him anymore. Now, I can recognize the path for what it is. Now, I snap the leash

depression. We have to change our expectations to reflect reality. Moving is a long process. Allow a full six months to a year to feel settled. Rely on family and long-term friendships for support.

3. *Stop analyzing.* Women are twice as prone to depression as are men. The primary reason is that women think too much. Don't keep analyzing why you can't get what you want when you *know* that line of thought depresses you. Don't give it a lot of thought. Moving is like walking across hot coals. Don't stop; keep going.

on that bad boy and haul him back up to normal life. I point out just where he went wrong, scolding the whole time. Black Dog piddles on the carpet.

Good. It's time for him to move on anyway. No one should be wandering around behind that creature, especially since depression is among the psychological problems most responsive to appropriate treatment. It's good to know that if I can't leash this dog myself, there are professional folks who can.

In an age before Prozac and Zoloft, Churchill dealt with his depression by seeking stimulating, zestful company. He avoided hospitals. He found solace in incessant activity, telling his family, "a change is as good as a rest." Then he would go off to paint pictures or lay bricks.

I'm no Churchill. It's enough for me to tell the Black Dog to lie down and go to sleep. It's enough to have a shorthand way of explaining to my family it's not them making me crazy, it's that durn dog. It's enough to know that one of these days, I'll be grilling a steak and look up, only to discover that the beast has gone and I am my own happy self again. Looking forward to it.

Roast a Chicken

Having a bad day? Having a really, really, wish-we-never-moved-hate-this-stupid-place kind of day? Then roast a chicken. I always do. It's better than Prozac for the unsettled soul. And a roasted chicken takes absolutely no culinary talent whatsoever. Rinse the bird off. Dig out its entrails (trés therapeutique). Stuff the cavity with an onion or a cut lemon and some rosemary and thyme. Add a little salt and pepper. Roast at 325 degrees for twenty-five minutes per pound. Baste. Because as you go about your chores, as you dig away at your life, the scent of Roast Chicken Love will fill your house. It smells so promising. So cozy. So darn homey, you can't help but feel your spirits lift. And it's good for at least two meals.

Spring at Last

Where thou art, that is home.
—Emily Dickinson

Just when you think you can't bear one more moment of winter, some crazy crocus rears its lovely head. That's the way it always goes. Just when you think you will never feel settled—you are.

I love that moment. Really, I do. I just wish that moment would ring the doorbell and let me know it has arrived. Instead, I'm usually going about the tasks of my little life and bump into it one day on the stairwell. How long have you been here? Come on in. What a surprise.

When the military member moves, he is almost instantly settled. He doesn't have to bump into his new life on the steps. He has brought his life and his identity across state lines. He wears his reputation on his chest. His new workmates take one look, ask a couple of questions, and know an awful lot about him.

It isn't the same when you are living on the Homefront. When we military spouses have reached this spring stage of the move, it's a major accomplishment. Because we haven't just moved the old life, like a little green house in a Monopoly game. We didn't pluck our lives off Oriental Avenue and push them over to Marvin Gardens, like it's no big deal.

A home and a life are living, breathing things. A seed planted and sown and transplanted. When you have nursed your new life, not just into living, not just into pushing out a few new leaves, but nursed it all the way into full bloom, you've really done something. Welcome home.

6 Military Brats

Is the Military Going to Wreck Our Family?

THEY SAY THAT NOVELIST Pat Conroy wrote the first definitive portrait of the American military family in his book *The Great Santini*. The central character, Colonel Bull Meecham, is the kind of Marine pilot who keeps the world Safe for Democracy. Based on Conroy's own father, Bull is a man's man. A hero, a despot. The kind of man who beats his wife. Drinks until knee-walkin' drunk. Bounces a basketball off his son's head. It is a family marked by loss, cruelty, silence, secrets, love, and the U.S. Marine Corps Hymn.

That is quite a family portrait to live up to. Or live down.

In her 1991 book, *Military Brats: Legacies of Childhood Inside the Fortress,* journalist Mary Edwards Wertsch fortifies that portrait with her analysis of the lifelong effects of the military on family members. The daughter of an Army colonel, Wertsch bases her description of the military community on five years of research and eighty interviews with military brats from both officer and enlisted families from all of the armed services.

I've never read a more frightening book in my life.

Written at a time when victimhood was strong in America and people claimed to be the adult children of just about anything, it slants in that direction. She characterizes the military as an invisible family member, "a secret controller who called the shots yet couldn't be challenged." Children are braced outside their rooms for white-glove inspections. Wives are secret alcoholics or trapped in loveless marriages or beaten every payday. Even the warrior fathers themselves are powerless and silent against the hand of the military.

Although I know individuals who swear Conroy's novel and Wertsch's study exactly describe their experiences, this kind of cruel warrior father was never part my life. My siblings and I can mimic accents with the best of them; we never braced for inspection. We never were called "troops" or "men" or "maggots." We never saw our father or mother drunk. My father, a fighter pilot, never in his life raised a hand in anger to any of us or to our mother.

He was not a perfect father. Talking to him is like pulling teeth. He never had much patience with spilled milk or algebraphobia. But my father was the benevolent presence reigning over our childhood. We were glad when he walked through the door at night. He loved us and our mother. He made us feel very, very safe.

The Eckharts were a military family, but the military was not a member of our family. The military was merely my father's choice—the way he chose to provide for his family. And, mercy, the man did love to fly.

The Military *Can* Change

The Conroy and Wertsch views of military family life are so negative they make you feel a fool for even trying to raise kids on the military's dime. According to them, the military shapes the warrior, and he, in turn, commits acts of war upon the family. So if the structure is so flawed, why try?

Because times have changed. Military life has changed—thanks partly to people like Conroy and Wertsch who pointed out how toxic and long-lasting the effects of military life can be on children. What makes things better now?

Generational Change

The clash depicted in these books is between two powerful generations—the Greatest Generation and the Baby Boomers—particularly over the Vietnam War. Add to this the heavy drinking and close scrutiny of the period, and you've got a mighty strong, potentially poisonous cocktail.

Change in the Role of Fathers

Military fathers of the Greatest Generation did not change diapers. They did not say "I love you" or go to the new duty station ahead of the family so their kids could finish the school year. Those things did not occur to them; they are pretty standard for fathers today. We require our servicemen to do their jobs, not bring them home.

Change in the Role of Mothers

Military wives in the past derived status and purpose through their husbands' jobs, but they had no money or power of their own. Most married women of the period did not work outside the home. If the marriage went bad, their options were extremely limited, both financially and socially. Yet their willingness to stay with an abusive mate caused real damage to their children. Now, both the military and the outside world offer programs to help families troubled by alcoholism and abuse. The court system also recognizes the military spouse's contribution by ensuring that he or she receives retirement income if there is a divorce. Leaving a toxic military marriage is difficult, but not impossible.

Change in the Role of Alcohol

When Conroy and Wertsch were growing up, drinking created bonds between strangers. Heavy drinking meant better stories, more craziness. It was accepted. It is less accepted today—there's less alcohol at official functions, at least. Today, we know that no matter how bad the alcoholism (or physical or sexual abuse) is before someone joins the military, the additional stress of military life makes it far worse.

We are doing better, much better, but our problem with alcohol isn't solved. One in thirteen Americans abuses alcohol. In the military, that figure is higher. In a 2004 survey conducted by the Department of Defense, 42 percent of the 12,500 military members surveyed admitted to binge drinking. They reported having at least five or more drinks on a single occasion at least once during the month before the survey. That rate is twice as high as the drinking rate among civilians. We need to work on that. How about starting now?

Change in Communication

Not only are we more open with our feelings, we also have more opportunities to express them than ever before—even when the service member is deployed. Previous generations were able to communicate only by letter; our generation has a whole range of options for keeping in touch. From cell phones to e-mail to instant messaging to cards and packages, service members have many opportunities to let their families know how much they love them, miss them, and long to come home.

There's No More "Hall of Mirrors"

Perhaps the most important change between our time and theirs is that the military has dismantled what Wertsch calls "the hall of mirrors." In earlier generations, a service member's family was seen as a direct reflection of his leadership ability. Officials endlessly scrutinized family members for these reflections at base schools and housing—even while they were mowing the lawn. From interacting more with the civilian community, we now understand that teenagers are teenagers and families are families. Hope for the best and get help for the worst. It's available.

Although many military families have problems (as do civilian families), we live and work in a kinder, gentler military. We breathe easier. It's a breath won on the backs of dependents like Pat Conroy and Mary Edwards Wertsch, who brought that past to life in a way that could not be ignored or denied.

So much has changed for the better. So much is still left to be done. We who live in the here and now can successfully raise our children within the military community. The goal of our generation is to find the best method possible.

What Can We Do for Our Kids?

I'm still hoping for a vaccination. I'm thinking these kids could just be inoculated against the effects of military life, rendered blind to long absences and deaf to commercials for expensive products. They could even get a big dollop of endorphins inserted into their systems with every move.

Until then, they've got us—a mom and a dad (and maybe a stepmom or a stepdad or a couple of really wonderful grandparents) standing between them and the painful parts of military life. We can do this. Fortunately, we don't have to do it all at once. Military life affects families in different ways at different times. It starts small and ramps up. We can't offer our children pain-free, vanilla lives. But we can and do help them effectively cope with everything that comes their way.

Babies and Toddlers

Babies and toddlers are ideal military family members. You can move a baby across fifteen time zones and she'll hardly notice. You can feed a toddler banana yogurt and a juice box in every state from Georgia to Alaska, and that kid won't care a bit. Babies have short memories, which ought to give us great peace. It doesn't. That short baby memory just makes us worry more than usual about bonding. Young (and not-so-young) moms worry that baby will forget Dad, whether he's gone for three weeks or eight months.

Guess what? Baby will definitely forget him. The good thing is that babies and toddlers won't hold it against him. They don't get mad if Dad leaves them in the loving (if overloaded) arms of Mom for a whole deployment. When it's all over, babies are generally glad to see anyone who is glad to see them.

Don't believe me? Ask around. Attend a Homecoming and witness any number of babies and toddlers reaching for daddies they didn't even know they had. After Dad's been home for a few weeks, you can hardly see a difference.

Moving, deployment, and Homecoming don't affect babies nearly as much as you might think. What really affects them is this: During those early years of a marriage, when a husband and wife are most intense about Becoming Parents, they also are the most intense about getting established in their careers. It's even more intense if one of those careers is stay-at-home mom. Stay-at-home dad? Katie, bar the door.

Achieving Baby Balance

Military life and baby life are two great things—two great things that do not go great together. In 2000, the Army released a study of 13,000 officers and family members revealing all of the usual dissatisfactions with military life. Junior officers surveyed felt alienated from senior commanders, overworked, and frustrated by an unpredictable life that disrupts families. Seventy-three percent of those surveyed said they were unable to achieve a proper balance between the Army and family life.

No kidding. Hasn't anyone told those guys in the Pentagon that there's no such thing as balance in family life when you've got babies, toddlers, or preschoolers running around? It isn't just 73 percent of Army officers who feel out of balance with their families, it's 73 percent of young families with children who feel out of balance.

Any young parent you ask will tell you: The minute you add that one little bitty baby, everything goes out of whack. It's like adding a sleeping bag to the whirling washing machine of your life. The load is instantly so unbalanced you can almost guarantee the Kenmore will be doing the ugly rumba across the laundry-room floor on a daily basis.

Babies do that to the lives of every parent—especially when the baby (or babies) is unexpected or not quite planned. Even though we of the birth-control generation think we can plan the arrival of our children, it doesn't always work that way. Is it any wonder that it takes a long time—the whole of our twenties and thirties, perhaps—to get work and kids and a reasonable love life into balance?

I think it must have taken me longer than most people to learn this lesson. I even went to a marriage counselor to complain that my young husband was not at all like my own father. Brad worked too much. He had the duty every third night. On the rare occasions when he was home, he was busy with his own weird stuff like edging the lawn and waxing the cars and watching the NCAA finals on TV. What kind of father was that?

The counselor never did answer this question. Instead, she told me to go to the wives of all the good fathers I knew and ask them what these men had been like when their children were young.

I did. My mother told me that my father as a young pilot was often "on alert," which meant he had to spend the night at the base so he could be airborne within five minutes. He did yearlong, unaccompanied tours in Vietnam and Korea. He did some night flying, took some trips. It wasn't until I was in school that he was home for dinner at six o'clock every night.

I tried to dismiss this temporary imbalance in their early life as just a product of the military. Then my Aunt Florence told me that my precious Uncle Jack worked long, hard hours at the steel mill when he was a young man. Even my grandmother said my grandfather, a farmer who never got tired of making jelly sandwiches for seventeen grandchildren, "thought you grandchildren were the first babies ever born. I wish he had paid some of that attention to his own four."

Oh.

It seemed it was the same all over. The more people I asked—young, old, military, civilian—the more I found that young fathers trying to get ahead in their careers worked a lot of hours. Balance for previous generations meant young men worked and young women stayed home raising children. Wives discovered life outside the home in middle age while their husbands discovered the wonder of grandchildren. Balance for them was achieved over a lifetime.

That wasn't the balance I wanted. I didn't want my husband to wait that long before he recognized childhood running swiftly by on size-three feet. No one does.

Today's military seems well aware that they must make some allowances for families. I think they try. But those new policies will not change the nature of the beast. Soldiers must go into the field; sailors must go to sea. Pilots must stand alert and fly at night and take the plane to Saudi Arabia on countless days of the year. Someone has to stand watch on Christmas day.

Young men and women with careers in the military must pay their dues to learn the job or we end up with a military force unprepared for the work at hand. Combining that role with fatherhood or motherhood is a task not to be taken lightly. But it gets easier over time. Hang on.

But What about the Baby's Mommy?

As hard as it is to balance work and family life for the military member, it is no easier on the Homefront. Even if you've been on the Homefront a long, long time. Maybe it's just part of being the mom.

My husband returned from one deployment when Peter was two months old. I was asleep on my feet.

"Why don't you go to bed, babe," Brad told me. "Baby's down. I got the kids. You should get some sleep."

"It won't happen," I said, my head swinging from side to side like a melon on a string. "I might get the baby to sleep. I might get the kids to direct all their questions to Daddy, the other awake parent. I might get you to stand in front of the bedroom door with a flaming sword like the archangel at the gates of heaven. But I'm not going to sleep."

"Why's that?"

Daddy Video

Babies are bizarre little people. They know more than we think they do. My husband deployed when my daughter was five months old. She barely ever saw him. But she would smack at an eight by ten picture we had of him and say "Da," as though she knew who he was. Kids this age like pictures of their dads. Laminate a bunch and throw them into the toy box. If you really want to thrill them, make a video of Daddy doing anything. Peter, our youngest, loves a video of Daddy coloring with him, Daddy pulling him in the wagon, Daddy reading *Dinosaur Roar*. Daddy is way cooler than Elmo.

"Cause I'm the pig," I said, with a little shuddering breath.

He looked up. "The pig? But you look great. You don't look like a pig."

"I didn't say I looked like a pig. I said I *am* the pig."

"How do you figure?" he said, switching off the computer and leading me to the bedroom.

"Remember how Pa kills the pig in *Little House in the Big Woods?*"

"No," he said. "Wasn't Michael Landon in PETA?"

I threw myself on the bed and covered my eyes with my arm. "Pa and the neighbor slaughter the pig at the beginning of the winter and Pa makes ribs and smokes hams. Then Ma cooks up the head for head-cheese, chops up the extra bits and pieces with sage for sausage, boils the bones to make glue. Mary and Laura get to roast the tail on a spit as a crispy treat, and then Pa blows up the pig's bladder and ties it with a string to form a fun ball for the girls to bat across the lawn."

Brad looked confused. "So you want us to make sausage?"

"No. I just feel like the pig. Every bit of the pig was used. Every bit of the pig was useful. Every bit of the pig was used up. About as used up as your average mommy."

"Dads get used up too." Brad protested, cuddling in around me.

"But not the same way as the mom. I've got people wanting my hands to roll out chicken pie. People who want my feet to press harder on the gas pedal. People who want my space on the kneeler in church. People taller than I am who want to sit in my lap. I've got a baby who likes Mommy's milk best, and since you got home there is a marked interest in bits of me that no one has wanted in at least seven months!"

He leered evilly at me. I shut my eyes, willing sleep. The baby started crying in another room. Brad got up. Our sixth grader took his place.

"Is Mom asleep? I need her to sign these three checks, write my social security number on this form, and help me look up that article on the Internet. It's due Tuesday. This Tuesday."

I breathed deeply, tried to snore a little. Then the second grader jumped on the bed. "Mom? Mom! I need to know: If ladies' breasts are meant to feed babies, what are men's nipples for?"

"Target practice," I snarled.

He laughed and examined his own chest. "No really, what are they for?"

Brad returned with Baby Pete in fresh jammies and diaper. "He needs you," Brad said. I sat up in bed ready to take him, suddenly remembering that a pig isn't just a hog in a pen, pork on the hoof, swine in the holler. A pig is also a Scottish word that means a vessel, a crock, a container that holds all there is to hold. Take good care of the pig—and the pig will take care of everything else.

Preschoolers

A reader once sent me an Internet list called "The Ways You Know You're a Military Family." According to that list, you know you're military when half of your closets are full of uniform stuff. When you pay thirty-five dollars to have a baby. When you can look at a base sticker and know the hometown of every person on the roster. Too true.

To me, the most telling "Ways You Know" weren't even on the list. I call them the "Ways of the Preschooler." The way your preschooler points to any airplane or military vehicle and says, "Daddy!" The way he vaguely believes his parent is anyone in uniform—regardless of race, gender, or branch of service. The way half of your family pictures feature some kid naked in combat boots.

Preschool kids have a way of thinking of their Parent in Uniform as Superman and Wonderwoman and Bob the Builder all rolled into one. It's a great time of life to be the one with the braid and the badges. It's a great time to be the dad.

At this stage, moves don't affect preschoolers too much. They are reasonably adaptable to a new environment. Their idea of time expands and collapses at will so the deployment seems like forever to them even if the separation lasts a week. The best thing we do for our kids at this stage is to set up good family practices. Every family is different. Eating together may be the most important thing you can do for your family.

The Family Dinner

The family dinner that makes people feel close is no Norman Rockwell portrait. Instead, it goes something like this: A chicken pie is browning nicely in the oven—*too* nicely. If Brad doesn't get home before seven thirty, he'll be eating a chicken-flavored hockey puck instead of his Grandma Betty's heirloom recipe.

Five-year-old Sam dashes into the kitchen, a bandanna tied rakishly around his head, an eye patch obscuring his vision.

"What have ye got to eat," he demands, brandishing his pirate sword.

"Dinner," I say firmly. "You can just wait for dinner."

"Aw, Mom," he whines, sucking in his bare belly. "I'm starving to *death*. When is Dad getting home?"

"Soon. Go play."

The doorknob rattles. Sam and I look at each other, then race for it. Before Brad steps all the way inside, I'm in his arms claiming First Kiss. Sam plows into his leg. The dog barks wildly at our feet.

"Daddy! Daddy! Daddy! Daddy!" Kelsey's bedroom door flings open and bangs against the wall. She runs downstairs and vaults onto him, all long arms and nine-year-old legs.

Homecoming around here tends to be painful. But joyous.

"Dinner is ready," I say, scrutinizing his still-crisp uniform. "Do you want to change?"

"No, it's late. Let's eat now."

We settle at the table, pass plates, say grace.

"So, how was your day?" Brad begins.

"Fine. I . . ."

"Thirty lashes and ye walk the plank," growls Pirate Sam.

"If you used a cat-o'-nine-tails, you'd only have to whip three times," chimes Kelsey. "See, nine times three is twenty-seven. Then whip three more times with a regular whip. *Then* make him walk the plank."

Kelsey preens. Sam eyes her warily. I sigh.

Like everyone else, I've read that family dinners are supposed to be good for us. Some researchers say that the single most important predictor of academic success is how often a family eats together. Others find that when families chat a lot during meals, kids tend to have larger word inventories.

We listen to Kelsey's "larger word inventory" as she describes the presidency of James Madison. Brad tells the kids a joke someone had e-mailed him. Sam rattles off the one about the sea monster's lunch. Again.

One of my friends says her Army husband hasn't been home for dinner in all of their fourteen years of marriage.

"He always works late," she confided. "Once, he was stationed at a base where the base commander declared Wednesday was family night. Everyone was supposed to leave the office at five o'clock and go home for dinner. But the boss didn't go, so no one else did either."

I paused, thinking of my friend and her three children eating alone, of all the parents I knew who get home just in time to kiss their kids good night. And yet there were plenty of families who found ways to share a meal together—breakfast, or lunches at elementary-school cafeterias, or desserts eaten when Dad came home at 9:00 P.M.

"Can I have a brownie now?" Sam interrupts. He nudges his not-so-flaky piecrust with his thumb.

"Drink your milk," Brad says automatically. "And sit all the way down in your seat."

For this endless sermon on good manners, Brad goes in at oh-dark-thirty, and/or skips lunch, and/or battles rush-hour traffic. He says if you come home late you have no interaction with the family. He says dinner is the turning point of the day. He says skipping dinner causes bitterness—friction that comes from putting one more thing ahead of the family.

I get up to fetch the plate of brownies from the kitchen and smile as they all cheer the arrival of dessert. As I glance from one face to another, I wonder how anyone could willingly miss this, the best part of the day. This exchange of silliness and good food and occasional snippets of adult conversation. This declaration of who we are as a family.

Sam giggles with the delight of chocolate on his tongue, his mouth open, his front teeth blackened with chewed brownie.

"Eww!" Kelsey and I groan together.

Sam leans against Brad's shoulder, still gleeful. His messy mouth smudges the pristine sleeve of Brad's uniform. Then, seeing what he has done, Sam kisses the sleeve to make it better.

"I guess I did need a clean uniform," Brad said.

"You do now," I answer.

Interpreter of His Absence

A man's life should be big enough to encompass both duty to family and duty to country. That can be a hard lesson for a boy to learn. It was a hard lesson for me. —Senator John McCain

Senator John McCain's father and grandfather were both four-star admirals. Yet, in his book *Faith of My Fathers: A Family Memoir,* McCain credits his mother as the one who taught him not only to take the constant disruptions of military life in stride but also "to welcome them as elements of an interesting life."

"As any other child would," wrote McCain, "I resented my father's absences, interpreting them as a sign that he loved his work more than his children." McCain (like many other military children) says now that he judged his father unfairly and that he regrets feeling that way.

He may be missing the point. A child's mind leaps to provide explanations for what it does not understand. My mother had the great virtue of profoundly understanding her husband. Once, when we were moving in the middle of a school year, I remember asking her why Daddy couldn't have a normal job "like an airline pilot" (as if that schedule would somehow be more normal).

"Oh, honeybunch," sighed this woman who had just spent a year alone with us while Dad had orders unaccompanied overseas, "that would be like asking Daddy to fly a bus. He loves to fly. You know that."

While I tried to picture my flight suit–clad father in the cockpit of the local school bus, Mom explained for the umpteenth time how Dad loved his work. How our father was a patriot. How he honestly believed it was his duty to serve our country. Later, when he only flew a desk, I remember Mom explaining that he was still working in the Air Force because we had three kids in college and two more to go, and his job was paying for all of that.

With those words and countless others, Mother prevented my brain from jumping to a conclusion that was not necessarily true—that Dad loved that plane more than me, more than my brothers and sister, more than my mother. She held open the place in which I would later judge my father, the way we all judge our fathers. She kept a spot for the time

Mommies Never Cry—Or Do They?

Sometimes a separation gets to be too much for even the best mom. A good cry into a bed pillow can help. But what if your kids catch you at it? Won't they worry? It's no big deal. Tell them you miss Daddy and that crying makes you feel better. Because it does. Hug them and hasten to assure them that you are a grown-up and you can handle this and take care of them. Mommies sometimes cry. And the sun still rises in the morning.

when I was mature enough to gather all the evidence, not just the evidence available to a ten-year-old.

My father and I will be forever grateful for that.

Now that I am the one at home, I am the Mighty Interpreter of Daddy's Absence. I could tell the kids anything. I could tell them Daddy didn't really have to work so many hours but that he was lazy and fooled around all the time. I could say the Navy doesn't care about families and that they make all the sailors work overtime on purpose. I could say Daddy has been abducted by the Dread Pirate Roberts and has to capture nine virgins before he's allowed to come home. And they would believe me.

But I don't. Instead, I tell them the same thing my mother told me. I tell them about the way the sun shines on the water when Daddy is at sea and how excited he is when he wakes up in sight of land. I remind them how he has papered his walls with their pictures from school. I tell them he misses them, that he loves them more than any job he will ever have. And I hold open a place for them to stand while they learn what it is to serve something greater—much greater—than yourself.

Elementary School

Things in the military family clip along at a crazy but emotionally manageable pace until kids start school. Then everything gets trickier. Because every school year that passes means that the kids have more of a life of their own, a life without you. I hate when that happens.

Sixty Minutes

Do you ever feel like you're just going to lose it with your kids? Like you've been a single parent long enough? Like these kids are a smidge away from being bent, folded, and mutilated into a size small enough to be sent to the ship or the field? Don't go there. Instead, imagine that Morley Safer just rang your doorbell. He's here to do a segment for *60 Minutes* about the Happy Military Family—and you're it. Pretend the cameras are watching; you'll be amazed how much patience you've got left in you.

Suddenly the moves and deployments are harder for kids to handle. Moves break up their friendships, their sports teams, the familiar comfort of their own bedrooms. Elementary school kids start to question why we have to move and why Daddy has to be gone. The deployments and separations mean they miss the interaction and advice and company of their father. Kids this age wish they could clone their dad so he could save the world *and* be home in time for dinner.

You and your husband love your kids like the sun. But during the elementary school years, you are often so far into the career that you feel like you can't quit without losing the retirement. This is where things get serious for the military child. We can transfer records and lobby for the gifted program and bring recommendations from coaches. But once you've done the conventional things, how do you clear their paths?

Her First Day

Everyone knows that moving to a new school is hard for a second grader from a military family. But I don't just *know* it. I was a military kid myself. I *remember* it. I remember walking to the new school in the dark and the rain and the way my kneesocks were wet inside my scuffed shoes.

I remember the way the fluorescent lights glinted off my new teacher's horn-rimmed glasses and one gold molar, making her look like a dead fish in a glass case. I remember not playing jump rope, not playing tetherball, not playing four square. I remember wandering the periphery of the playground every day, promising myself hotly that I would love my children too much to *ever* make them move.

But the brain is a pattern-making, pattern-repeating device. I married the only military guy I ever dated and we have moved and moved and moved. Then, in the middle of second grade, we moved our daughter. And I found myself back on my old battlegrounds, a little scarred, but better armed.

For my daughter, I started a campaign that would rival MacArthur's return to the Philippines. I asked Kelsey's teachers to write letters of recommendation. We made a special trip to her new school to meet the principal. I helped her send a letter and photo to her new class. We planned a farewell party, bought new notebooks, took Kelsey on a tour of the school. Every student in Kelsey's new class not only wrote her back, they each drew a self-portrait as well.

All was ready for the Storming of the Second Grade.

D-Day dawned with Kelsey up-and-at-'em by 0630, dressed in her new black jumper with the purple turtleneck and purple tights and purple headband—the second-grade equivalent of a power suit. She tingled with excitement, brimmed with confidence, carefully held her little brother's hand as we crossed the street in front of the school.

I was confident too. Who wouldn't want this kid for a student, a classmate, a best friend?

At the elementary school we got caught up in the swirl of students streaming into classrooms. Outside the second grade, everyone lined up against the wall. A girl in a blue coat caught sight of us and pointed. "Kelsey!"

The other kids took up the call and shouted, "Kelsey! Kelsey! You're here!"

A bevy of little girls flocked around her. I noticed that my daughter was a full head taller than every girl in this class. Kelsey kept walking toward the classroom door, perplexed about why they weren't just going in.

"No! No! You have to get in line!" the girls called, holding their places with one Keds-clad toe on the tile floor. Kelsey turned, but couldn't figure out where the end of the line was.

"How old *are* you, anyway?" one girl asked.

"I'm seven," Kelsey said coolly. The girls exchanged looks. I reached for Sam only to find him nine yards away, playing in the water fountain. When we got back to the classroom, the new teacher greeted us right at the door. She sent Kelsey to the back of the room with some other kids to hang up her coat and bag.

"Nice meeting you," I mumbled awkwardly, craning my neck. I glimpsed Kelsey darting sideways glances at the other kids, trying to figure out the routine. She slowly opened her backpack and slowly took out her unicorn notebook, her sharpened pencils, her glue. Her little face filled with trepidation.

"Good-bye," the teacher said brightly, nudging me out. "I'm sure she'll be fine."

I'm not, I thought to myself. *I'm not sure she'll be fine.*

I wanted to push past this teacher and grab my little girl. I wanted to hold her, hug her, take her home, wrap her up so nothing would ever hurt her. How could I ever have thought I could protect her from moving to a new school? I may campaign with the best of them, but in the end this was *her* battle that she had to fight alone. And I'd armed her only with a purple headband, a unicorn notebook, and a sunny disposition.

The teacher turned away, but I could not. I pushed Sam forward. "Did you kiss Sissy good-bye?"

He darted past the teacher, ran into Kelsey's arms the way baby brothers are allowed to do. She kissed the top of his head and turned away. I let myself breathe. Then I took Sam's hand and walked back up the long dark hallway.

Birds and Trees

The whole thing about moving kids from place to place always makes me think of that snappy poster—the one that says really good parents give their children roots *and* wings. I know it's meant to convey the idea that you have to raise your kids in a solid home with solid morals, and then give them the freedom to be themselves and fly away.

In real life, things work out in a more physical way. Give them roots and wings? It can't be done. The way I see it, either you raise your kids in one—maybe two—places and they have roots, or you give them the joys and horrors of moving around, and they have wings. You get the benefits of one or the other. Not both. You plant trees or you raise birds.

But lately I've been thinking that we grown birds and trees don't seem to understand each other very well. To continue to push this silly metaphor a little further, birds seem to annoy the very leaves from the trees. I can see why. Birds don't seem to earn their place in the forest. They aren't related by blood or acorn to any of the other inhabitants. They don't put down the kind of roots that help the forest fend off strong winds. They just appear one day, building nests in tree branches. Their birdlings divert all kinds of attention from the saplings. And then, just when you get used to them, just when you start liking them, they're gone.

No wonder birds are so unpopular. On the other hand, trees don't seem to understand how we birds look up to them. How we envy their roots, their forests, their imperturbability. How so many of us would love to be them.

Yet trees go on taking their kids on vacation, hoping that it qualifies in the wing department. Birds hustle their children off to visit the grandparents in the summer and put up the same painting above the same couch in every house—from sea to shining sea—hoping it qualifies as roots.

Maybe it would be simpler just to change the silly saying. Trees can say, "We want to give our children roots, *then* wings." And birds can say, "We give our children wings so they can *find* roots."

We can only try.

Childhood Friends

Grown-up military brats all complain about the same things. They say they're not "from" anywhere, that their fathers missed too many birthdays, and that they missed having childhood friends.

I am only one woman. I cannot fix all those things. But I can do something about providing my kids with childhood friends—I can make them a priority.

My son, Samuel, and his buddy, Forrest Peterson, have known each other since preschool. Our families have driven across town, across state, and up and down the East Coast making sure these boys have playdates. Sam and Forrest have eaten their "traditional meal" in every single house we've lived in—score four (4) for the Navy family and five (5) for the Marine Corps family.

That's a lot of hot dogs. That's a lot of macaroni and cheese.

But we think it's worth it. We think it's important for children to have at least one friend who remembers playing in their backyard. One friend who played Batman to their Robin. One friend at their wedding who can still picture them with hair—any hair. How can a parent make that happen?

Get lucky; work hard. A lifelong friendship must be child driven. Just because your best girlfriend has a kid the same age as yours doesn't mean the kids will be palsy-walsy. If your kid makes a true friend, plan to make the most of it. Make friends with those parents. When you move, get street addresses, e-mail addresses, phone numbers. Stay in touch. *You* are the fuel in this engine. Not the kid, not the other parent. You.

Be in the Navy or Marine Corps. Unlike the Army, Air Force, or Coast Guard, we Navy and Marine Corps families seem to have fewer bases and more opportunities to be stationed together again. At the very least, we always seem to live in places where the parents of our kid's friends want to go on vacation. Many families make it a tradition to vacation between the two duty stations.

Expect age-appropriate effort. When they first moved away from each other, Forrest and Sam did not e-mail, call on the phone, or write letters. They were five years old. They had busy little lives of their own. But every so often they mentioned each other, wished for each other. We didn't talk them out of it. We parents always agreed that Forrest (or Sam) was a truly great friend. That's all that was required.

Send pictures. Children are visually oriented. A picture of a friend in a Halloween costume, at the pool, or making a silly face tells the whole story. Send a picture once or twice; that's plenty.

Jump at the opportunity. If an opportunity to get together pops up, leap on it. Even if the chance happens once in three years. Even if it isn't quite convenient. Forrest and his family happened to be driving through Norfolk the same day I happened to go into labor. We still invited them over—which is Sam's best memory of the day. Mine too.

Balance tradition with new experiences. Every friendship is cemented by familiar activities. When Kelsey and Meghan (a fourth-grade friend) visited, they just had to stay up all night watching movies and talking. But they also added new memories to the mix with a trip to the Washington Monument and lunch (hot dogs!) at the White House.

Let the friendship evolve. The window for a childhood friend to walk through is narrow. No matter how great the friendship starts out, sometimes kids outgrow each other. The friend you had at four might not be the friend you want at fourteen. Enable, but don't enforce.

Sam and Forrest have taught each other many things: how to jump on a trampoline, how to play lacrosse, how to fight with sticks without getting caught. But mostly they are teaching each other that moving doesn't mean you lose everything. Moving doesn't mean you have to lose friends.

Bathtub Full of Pain

When I come upon a child crying, particularly my own child crying about an upcoming move or a too-long separation, my first thought is to *hush him up.* But I don't. Trying to talk children out of their pain never, never works. Instead, think of your dear child as an overflowing bathtub. Instead of trying to shut off the waterworks, be sure to open the drain. Let the kid talk all he wants about how he misses Daddy or how he's sure he'll never find another friend. Affirm what he says. Tell him that you miss Daddy too. Agree how much it must hurt to lose a friend like Forrest. And then *shut up.* People—even little people—want to feel heard and understood. The more you listen, the more they feel their worries escape down the drain without leaving a ring.

House of Gals

Second-grader Sam stalked into the kitchen one day in January, placed a firm hand on my arm, and announced, "We *will* be watching the Superbowl on Sunday."

"Oh, yeah?" I said, turning to give him the full brunt of Mommy's Evil Eye. The boy wasn't asking, begging, pleading, groveling, or any of the other things I like to hear from small children. "Why do you think we'd do that?"

He looked me full in the face and said, "Because that's What Men Do."

Properly chastised, I backed off. In a House of Deployment, we don't get to see a lot of What Men Do. Not only had we missed every football game of the season, I hadn't even realized it was Superbowl Sunday until I saw all the chili and hot wings recipes in the newspaper. Dang.

"I guess that would be okay," I said slowly. "Who are you rooting for?"

"Dad says the Rams. So I'm going for the Rams. He says on the ship the game starts at three in the morning. Can I stay up that late? And can we have peanuts and popcorn too?"

I kept a straight face, resolving to e-mail Brad on the ship about how cute his kid is. But would he get it?

During this deployment the two guys in our family, who used to be close enough to accidentally appear in matching khakis and golf shirts, seemed so much farther apart. While deployment causes distance in every relationship, my daughter and I can use words to fill in the gaps between Brad and us. E-mail from the ship is the greatest blessing for me. Kelsey sometimes writes to her dad, but more often, she saves up her thoughts for our weekly phone call.

But our Sam is a man. Or at least a male of the species. He's not as verbal as his sister. He doesn't cry much. When we offer to plumb the depths of his feelings about the deployment, Sam looks at us like we've offered to let him try on a pair of pantyhose. "I miss Dad" is about as deep as it gets with him.

At predeployment briefs, we are reminded that kids, especially boys, don't always talk about their feelings. Instead, they act out in school, let their grades slip, change their behavior. We scarfed up all the literature they had about keeping sailors and kids feeling close. Even though the suggestions are inventive, they don't seem to work with our boy. He's not big on drawing pictures. He types on the computer only when he has to. His portion of the phone call consists of saying, "I love you, Dad. Miss you. Want to talk to Mom?"

I guess I shouldn't be surprised. The male-to-male relationship this father-and-son team has going is just like every other male relationship I know about. While women friends are insulted if they don't hear from you every third day, my husband's high school and college buddies don't call him for years. Then, they pick up the phone or run into each other at Lowes and instantly attain the same level of friendship they had when they last spoke seventeen years ago.

Sam's relationship with his father is about doing, not talking. They do stuff together. Bag leaves, play ball, watch each other's games. Eat, go to church, clean stuff, use wrenches.

Perhaps that's why the deployment seems harder for Sam than for the rest of us. There isn't any *doing* going on. In this abode of women (including the effeminate dog), we females want to talk, emote, feel, analyze, discuss. But Sam only wants to do. His relationship is frozen until Dad comes back.

During that Superbowl, the boy was a joy to behold. When it looked like the Rams were going to pull it out after those last two touchdowns, he marched around the living room, scrambling over the backs of couches in unmitigated glee. He downed enough ginger ale to give himself a hangover the next day. And when the Patriots won, he went out and sat on the porch, brooding.

He hadn't been out there two seconds before the phone rang. Sam ran inside to pick it up. "Hello? Dad?!"

It poured out of him—out of them both, perhaps. All of the reasons why the Rams didn't win. Bad plays. Bad luck. Curses on the kicker and the time clock. The boy walked around on his tippy toes, talking into the cordless for longer than he'd ever talked before.

I'm not a big fan of football; I would never have rolled out of my rack at 3 A.M. to watch a silly game before a full day's work. For that one moment of shared experience between father and son, though, I'll bless the NFL forever.

Teenagers

During peacetime, deployment for a teenager means one fewer driver to take you to swim practice, pick you up from the movies, shoot foul shots. It means you've got a mom who is even more irrational, emotional, and flat-out uncool than ever.

As long as mom holds the line on family rules and there isn't an actual war on, teens can hold it together during deployment. It's moving that kills a teenager. Because they aren't just losing their rooms, their whole lives disappear.

Reputation

I didn't know there was a problem until the parent/teacher conference. At that conference, the team of three seventh-grade teachers asked Kelsey how she "felt" when she saw her grades.

"Ummm, fine," she said, darting a glance at me. "I earned what I got and I . . . um . . . guess I'll have to . . . uh . . . study the vocabulary a little better in Spanish? Because I can't . . . um . . . pro-nun-si-kate it that good?"

"That is pro-nun-ci-ATE," the English teacher said, picking up Kelsey's report card. A look of surprise darted across her face. "This is a very good report card."

Teens and War

When their fathers or mothers are deployed to a war zone, you can't placate teenagers. You can't just tell them everything will be all right and leave it at that. Teens have a way of flipping on CNN after school, memorizing the name of their parent's unit, and worrying about everything privately. They are more grown up than we know.

Deal with their emotions as though they were adults. Teach them to handle this kind of anxiety—learn about it together. Know what makes your teen feel most loved and do it: Spend time talking. Go to a movie, or anything else she loves. Give little gifts. Hug her. Most importantly, teach her to turn off the TV. We will know what we know when we know it. Don't hunt up trouble.

Kelsey and I exchanged looks. Of course it was a good report card. It is always a good report card. Obviously, something else was going on here. But what? Surely her navel is fully covered during school hours. She rarely, if ever, smells of burning hemp. Grown men do not call our house asking for Lolita.

"She is quite a talker," her math teacher intoned, lips pressed together. "Well, you see, that's because I'm really a blonde," Kelsey riffed. "I may have brown hair, but I'm tellin' ya, my roots are blonde."

And then I knew. The junior high goofiness that popped up in Kelsey and her girlfriends at her old school was being taken at face value at her new school. These new teachers thought her good grades were a *fluke,* as if I should be astounded, as if I had called down a miracle from heaven above and perhaps we should notify the pope having been thus visited.

Unbelievable, but true. Although Kelsey had been a good student since day one (and her record said so), she was an unknown entity at this school. She had no reputation. Her new teachers did not think of her as the kind of girl who could read in kindergarten. They didn't know how she was despised as teacher's pet in fourth grade. They were not amazed that she could drive the ball down the court without her knees knocking together. They couldn't picture her with bangs.

They saw only what they saw. She was a new kid. She had no reputation. It wasn't a question of having a bad reputation or losing a good reputation, but living without any reputation at all. She floated free of her past mistakes, but she was also unanchored, unweighted, unsustained by her past accomplishments.

It's hard enough for parents to start over, reputation free. It is so much harder for a teenager—especially one who expects to make the basketball team with ease, or has always been the first-chair trumpet. It's just as tough on the teen who won the science fair three years running, or has a sense of humor that won't quit.

Breaking in a whole new set of people, showing them who you are and what to expect from you, ain't no joke. It's a lesson most people learn at college, or when they take a new job. It's grown-up work. But each time we move, we expect it to be performed by people barely old enough to know who they are. We parents do our best to support them. But they're the ones who bear the load.

High School Move

It's hard to imagine why anyone would want to move a teenager. Move *away* from a teenager, yes. But actually move to a new place *with* a teenager? Who wants that? Our teen is lucky we let her come along.

Our teen does not exactly see it that way. Her idea is that we have moved enough. If Dad gets orders, she thinks she'll be real cute with her own apartment right here. Which is funny, because I think she'd be real cute doing time at a military school.

Our friends Bob and Kathy McKenna came up with a solution that actually helps teenagers embrace a move. When they announced their move, their son Bobby announced his decision to stay. Bob and Kath told him he would be allowed to pick his own high school in their new town. They felt he was old enough to look around at different schools in the area himself. They said they would choose a house *after* Bobby had picked the school.

Which, at first thought, sounded like a very expensive proposition. But they didn't make it open season. They didn't offer him a choice of any school in the county. That school with the cannabis-leaf wallpaper and the one with the shiny new methamphetamine lab were strictly off limits. Bobby was allowed to consider only schools that met his parents' criteria, in neighborhoods they could afford. They pledged to go with his decision.

Bobby still wasn't thrilled about moving. But when he went to visit, he took an instant liking to one of the schools—especially after talking to the cross-country coach. Back home, he actually started looking forward to the new school; it seemed better than the old one. Imagine.

Could that work for us? Like all military parents, we want our kids to be happy—despite the move. We want them to have what they want. But aside from unconditional love and carte blanche at the mall, what is it that she wants, really?

Control. Dominion. Sway.

More than anything else, teens seem to want power over their own lives. Can you blame them? When it comes to choosing between relatively equal schools, aren't they the best judge?

Moving a High School Senior

The number one Worst Thing military parents can do is move a high school senior. Unless the kid is very unhappy at his old school, this rarely works out well. By the time kids reach eighteen, they've done enough for their country. This is one of the few times when it makes sense for a service member to do a tour as a geographic bachelor.

"But what if I mess it up?" Kelsey asked when we told her that she would be going to our new duty station to look at schools. "What if I pick the school and I'm wrong?"

"So you make a mistake. Big Deal. Mistakes can almost always be rectified. It won't ruin your life. You can do this."

We military people always seem to do things in the same order. We move to a new place, choose a school system, pick our house, and inform the kids where they're going to attend school. While this is perfectly appropriate with elementary school kids, it loses its charm as kids get older.

Look at them. They're bigger than we are. They have changed since the last time we moved. And perhaps we need to change the way we deal with them.

If the Military Is So Hard on Kids, Why Doesn't He Just Get Out?

Despite the back problems that plagued him, when forty-year-old Cal Ripken Jr. announced his retirement from the Baltimore Orioles after twenty-one seasons, he said he was doing it for his kids. "The last couple of years I've been noticing that I miss being away from home," he told reporters. "I miss my kids' activities . . ."

I have an inkling that when the Iron Man mentioned he was choosing to spend more time with his family, wives of baseball players everywhere felt a cold sliver of doubt creep around the edges of their lives. After all, when a man of honor like Cal Ripken Jr. leaves his lucrative work in favor of his family, it makes you wonder about your own man of honor.

Does he love us as much as he loves that job?

We military families grapple with the same question all the time. It's one of the central questions of our lives. At a reunion we attended a few years ago, I talked to many of our friends who had left the military. After these guys mentioned what they're now driving and dropped hints about how much they now earn, they each looked deeply into my eyes and said, "Really, I left because of the wife and kids. I just couldn't see leaving the family so much. I was missing everything. It isn't worth it."

Not "It *wasn't* worth it." Or "It isn't worth it *to me.*" Just "It isn't worth it." As if it isn't worth it to anyone. A stone grew in my chest when I heard that. My inner voice whispered that these guys, these really good guys, loved their families so much that they couldn't deploy or do workups or have duty nights ever again. *These men love their families more than Brad loves us.*

By the time I called my mother that night, I was in tears. But my mother—an Air Force wife for twenty-five years—understands many things better than I ever will.

"Honey, when a man says he is leaving the military because of his wife and kids, that is an answer to which there is no argument," she said. "Who would dare say that a job is more important than a child? No one."

"So it's just an excuse?" I sniffled.

"No, not an excuse. But it is only part of the reason. When it comes to making decisions about work—especially work that requires a lot of travel—a man puts his life on a scale. On one side of the scale are the things he gets from his career—his paycheck, how much he likes the actual job, how well he is doing. On the other side of the scale are the things he gets from his family."

"Yeah, like dinner? Like laundry?"

"Not so much dinner," she laughed, "and definitely not laundry. But a man who is doing well at his work and sees that his family does pretty well with his absences weighs his life in a different way than a man who is not being promoted, or a man who hates his job, or a man whose family falls apart if he is gone only for a few days."

"He does?"

"Yes, he does. The man whose family does pretty well weighs his life and his job and finds that the two balance each other. He thinks that it's worth it—even though he probably pines for his wife and kids the whole time he is away. The other man weighs the unfulfilling job against the family and finds that it's not worth it. And he gets out and finds another job."

"So it doesn't mean the guy who leaves the military loves his family more?" I asked.

"No," she said firmly, "it really doesn't. Don't judge your husband based on how much travel the job requires. Instead, notice how he acts with all of you when he is home."

That is the message for us and the message we want to send our children. To take note of all the things your husband does for you and your family. Does he love coming home? Does he show his kids he loves them? Does he do laundry or pick up shin guards on his way home from work? Is he reliable, generous, hardworking, kind, devoted? Does he want the best for your family?

A family is all about give and take. Remind your children about the many ways their father gives to his.

7 Family

Yours, Mine, and Ours

For this reason a man will leave his father and mother and cleave unto his wife, and the two will become one. —Genesis 2:24

Parents

ON MY HONEYMOON, I cried from Ohio to Tennessee. This perplexed my twenty-three-year-old bridegroom. Brad thought he had spent the past twenty-four hours making me very, very happy. Heavens, he had done his work. I was happy—embarrassingly happy. Happy to be married to Fabulous Him. Happy we had such a lovely white wedding. Happy we were finally starting our real life together.

But once we crossed the Ohio River, I could not stop the tears from seeping out of my head. Because it wasn't until the very moment my parents kissed me good-bye that I realized becoming Brad's wife meant I wasn't going to be their little girl ever again. At twenty-one, I honestly thought I would always be their little girl. In some ways, at thirty-eight, I still am. I can still hold their hands when we walk together, I still can bounce on their bed to kiss them good night, and I can still get a thrill when I steal sodas out of their fridge. But after my marriage, I was not really their little girl anymore.

In addition to being my own self, I was *his* girl. Brad's girl. Brad's wife. And, in the language of my family, that meant he came first. This . . . this . . . this *stranger* came before my parents. They knew it, I knew it, and they knew I knew it.

We all noticed that my daughterly devotion wasn't stopping me from getting into the honeymoon car loaded with wedding presents, though. It wasn't stopping me from heading off to Brad's duty station in Orlando. But it hurt terribly to give up that very safe little-girl life.

Some military brides are like me, young and in love and idealistic enough to believe strictly in happily-ever-after. Other brides are only too happy to escape their wacky families. Other older brides are fully aware of the adult job and adult life they are letting go in the name of one man in uniform.

No matter where you come from, something about marrying a military man often makes the break between portions of your life very sharp and very clear—whether you marry at seventeen, twenty-one, or thirty-five. You not only marry into a new way of life, you also often move far, far away from home at the same time.

Is Moving Away from Family Bad for Me?

I can't ever decide whether that fast, hard break is good or bad for a marriage. In some ways, it stresses the marriage because there is no family support for a very young relationship. And our marriages in the early years do need supporting.

In other ways, the sharp geographic break helps cement the relationship. Nothing focuses a couple on its you-and-me-against-the-world-ness than starting a new life in a new place together.

As much as I love my parents, I credit the separation from them as necessary to my womanhood. I am not a terribly energetic person. I am not a go-getter. I'm more of a stay-homer and be comfortable-er. What would have happened to me if I had married a hometown boy? Or insisted that Brad become a hometown boy?

At my niece's baptism several years ago, I found myself reflecting on just that question. I was sitting at one end of the pew with eight-year-old Kelsey. My four-year-old son slept in my husband's arms. My parents settled behind us.

At the other end of the pew, my brother Dan and his wife, Karen, were getting their baby ready for the ceremony—pulling the family baptismal gown down over her ruffled white socks, hunting up the extra pacifier, smoothing her wisps of dark hair.

Baby Madeline was too busy flirting with my father to pay any attention to her parents. She started kicking her feet, waving her arms, dimpling and looking away, then looking back at him again to see if he was watching her. He was. As usual.

I turned away, trying to ignore the gnaw of envy. Envy. Like my parents had not blessed me all my life. Like I still had to have every drop of their attention. But what else could I call the feeling I had every time I noticed how involved my parents were with their newest grandchild?

Since my brother and his family live only a mile from my parents, they naturally see a lot of each other. They spend Sunday afternoons watching football together and they sing together with the Dayton Philharmonic. My parents babysit a few hours a week so that Karen can hold onto her part-time job. My parents kept baby Madeline so her parents could go to church, the grocery, or out to dinner.

My brother often says he chose that house on purpose—because he wanted my parents to be involved in his family. I can hardly blame him. I would have loved some help from my parents.

When Kelsey was baby Madeline's age, Brad deployed. Although my parents were constantly available for love, support, and advice by phone, 656 miles was too far for babysitting.

That year was my Trial by Fire. On the one hand, I was overwhelmed by the love I felt for my tiny baby girl. I would wake up in the morning and bring her into my bed to cuddle, marveling at the way her nose wrinkled when she laughed, at the trust in her soft brown eyes, at the sweet curve of her lip.

On the other hand, I was dismayed by the responsibility. What if I was doing it all wrong? What if I forgot her in the grocery cart? What if she stopped breathing? During nights when Kelsey wouldn't stop crying, I used to fantasize about handing her to Brad on the brow of the ship, shouting, "She's your baby now!" I'd turn on my heel and sprint away—possibly forever.

I would have done anything that year to be able to hand my child over to the loving care of my parents, to be released—even for a little while—of that staggering responsibility.

My parents invited me to come home to visit, and I did go home for a couple of weeks. But we all knew my home wasn't in Dayton anymore. The ship wouldn't come sailing up I-75 and dock on my parents' porch. If Brad and Kelsey and I were going to be a military family, I had to be able to live through the constant separations. I had to be able to make a happy home for my daughter. And I had to do it far from the comforting arms of my family—no matter how gut-wrenching it would be.

So I did. Don't picture me sallying forth and being brilliant at it every day and every hour. Instead, picture me slogging through it one day at a time. Attending Jazzercise classes just because they had baby-sitting and grown-ups there. Eating burgers with my friend Jeanne. Calling my parents on the phone. Sleeping with the light on.

At the end of that deployment, at the end of every challenge the military has offered me, I looked up and discovered I was a different person. Stronger than I would have been had I stayed home. Far more accomplished. Perhaps—if this is possible—more married. The way my husband seemed more married, more melded, more bonded to me.

Without trying to be too two-paths-diverged-in-the-woods-y, I do wonder sometimes what would have happened without this military life. It could be that I would have been exactly the same woman, in a safe little life in a safe suburban world. But I doubt it. Change is the only sure thing in life. And a step toward a more independent, stronger you is a step toward a better life.

They Are Still My Parents

My father said nothing when he saw the nine bruises I had earned by lugging boxes marked "dolls" from cellar to attic. My father ignored the three scratches I acquired scootching boxes marked "long tools" from attic to cellar. My father even managed to refrain from commenting when the movers dented my car. But the Kenmore dryer he found dumped at the bottom of the cellar steps was just too much for him.

"Daughter," he said, "this has not been a good move."

No kidding, Dad. I followed him down the steps and squeezed past the dryer for the third time that day. I would have moved the dryer earlier, but the mound of boxes, curtain rods, and free-range power tools left no room for Jell-o, much less major appliances.

Dad picked up a load of fishing rods and began threading them through the rafters. I moved to the far corner and stripped open another box. My fingers were cracked and swollen and aching from the harsh cleaners I'd been using all week.

I wanted to cry. Not because this move was rapidly heading for the Mover's Wall of Infamy. I wanted to cry because my father was here witnessing the way my life was actually going. Earlier that week, when my tragedies were reaching Jonah proportions, Mother had called, offering to send Dad to help me. Since she was working and Brad was still at school in Rhode Island, Dad, with his drill strapped to his hip, seemed the best solution.

I hesitated.

It wasn't that Dad was hard to please, difficult to get along with, or unkind in his remarks. And anyone brave enough to enter the Twilight Zone of our family move was a blessing. It was just that my father is the one person on earth I want to impress. Because he has always impressed me.

From my earliest memory of him coming across the tarmac, tall and tan in his flight suit, I have wanted my father to admire me. To think I'm smarter than I really am. Wittier, prettier, more organized.

Although my mother is allowed to know about my feet of clay, I didn't want my father to see for himself that under my leadership, things get stepped on, broken, thrown away. That only half my cabinets have shelf paper. That I dread confronting the landlord about the unpainted trim.

"Honey," Mother said, breaking in on my thoughts, "fathers can do very little for their grown-up, married daughters. Don't you remember how Grandpa used to come over to help me when Dad was stationed in Thailand? You need help. Let your father come and help you."

So I did.

Dad cleared a spot for the dryer and we shifted it into place. In an hour, we managed to find the box of tools, locate the right kind of nails, and negotiate some basement work space.

We worked well together, though we never had before.

That night, I put the kids to bed while Dad fussed with the fans and air conditioners, trying to maintain a comfortable temperature in Kelsey's attic bedroom. I collected wet socks from the bathroom, started a load of laundry, flipped on the dryer.

In the now-organized living room, Daddy sat with his size-thirteen feet propped on the ottoman, the crossword puzzle on his knee, his chin bobbing on his chest. He was sleeping. I sat across from him and lined my little feet up against his. The hum and tumble of drying clothes was the only sound in the room. And the goodness of being this man's daughter—needs and wants and strengths and flaws—filled my house from attic to cellar.

Raising the Out-of-Town Grandchild

Sit around the base pool long enough and moms eventually get around to the Thousand Inadequacies of the Grandparents. Poor old people. Even if they spend exactly the same amount on Christmas and birthday gifts, bend over backwards when the military grandchild visits, and traipse through three airports to get to your new duty station, they still can't overcome the In-Town/Out-of-Town Grandchild Syndrome.

The fact is, the grandchild who lives in town, whose diapers get changed on grandma's couch, whose preschool assemblies and soccer matches are grandfather attended, is different than the Out-of-Town grandchild. The In-Towners aren't more loved or less loved. They are just more *witnessed*. That can make the military parent feel edgy and left out.

The different nature of these relationships doesn't have to be a big deal unless we parents make it into one. When I was growing up, I loved visiting my grandparents once or twice a year. My cousins lived next door to them. But it never occurred to me to think Grandmother and

> **The Highway Runs in Both Directions**
>
> It's rewarding to attend events back home, but be sure to let your parents, siblings, nieces, nephews, and cousins into your life too. Invite them to your military events—graduations, commissionings, air shows, retirement ceremonies—as well as your children's baptisms, first communions, plays, games, matches, and recitals. Centering a family visit on these kinds of activities makes things run more smoothly.

Grandfather could possibly love the In-Towners more. We Out-of-Towners were so precious to them, so worthy of little cards and letters, so welcome when we visited, that I could not imagine anyone being loved more.

At my grandmother's funeral, each of the cousins—In-Towners and Out-of-Towners—stood up and said how we were each Grandmother's favorite. We were. The relationship between grandparents and grandchildren can't be weighed and measured like Brach's candy at the grocery. It's an exponential thing. Don't ruin it by trying to get it all.

Dealing with the In-Laws

Of all the many experiences I have to look forward to in my adult life, the one I am dreading the most is becoming a mother-in-law. Could there be a role for which I am less suited? A mother-in-law has to have tact. She has to have wisdom. She has to have the ability to keep her opinions to herself!

I'm doomed.

When I think of adding the emotional rigors of military progeny to an already-volatile mix—I quake with fear.

Not many parents-in-law seem to handle the military with aplomb. Why would they? Fewer and fewer Americans have firsthand experience with the military. The military guy doesn't just marry their daughter; he whisks her off to the scraggliest corners in the world and *leaves her there.*

Making a daughter cry is hardly gonna win a popularity contest with her parents.

Most parents and parents-in-law seem to make their biggest mistakes during the period surrounding a deployment. They don't visit you enough or they visit you too much. They drown you with help, or they don't seem to think you need any at all.

I'm very fortunate. My own parents-in-law seem to have second sight when it comes to dealing with our military life—especially when it comes to deployments. Although Larry and Judy have never been affiliated with the military themselves, their only son joined the Navy and their only daughter married into it. Somehow, they have learned to time their pre- and post-deployment visits perfectly, offer plenty of support to the families at home, and stay on excellent terms with their sailors at sea.

Here are ten secrets about deployment to pass along to your in-laws—no, strike that. Pass these tips on to your own parents; let your husband pass them along to the in-laws long before the deployment begins.

1. *Understand that the deployment starts being stressful even before it begins.* You would think that the stress of a deployment does not begin until the plane leaves the runway, the ship leaves the port, or the sub heads out to sea. Not so. Since workups consume much of the six-month period before the deployment, couples are already stressed out thirty days before the ship leaves. Consider this normal. Behave accordingly.

2. *The workload in the battalion or on the ship itself is burdensome.* Remember your child during exam week? Although he had plenty of time to finish his ten-page term paper on *Beowulf* during the semester, I bet he was up the night before it was due writing, cramming for a chemistry exam, and packing his bag to leave the next day. Even though that guy is now a military man, he (and the rest of his detachment) still has repairs to complete, supplies to on load, and paperwork to turn in—not to mention mulch to spread and a swing set to build at home. Send cookies during this time.

3. *Know that every issue in your child's marriage will be bubbling up.* Deployment doesn't necessarily cause problems for military couples, it just turns up the heat on all the pots that are already bubbling away on the marital stove. Even the most loving couples have spats. You don't really want to witness this.

4. *Visit before the thirty-day countdown.* When someone you love is going to be out of the country for six months or more, it's natural to want to visit just before he leaves. Don't do it. Instead, try to plan your visit more than thirty days before your child deploys. Play holidays by ear.

5. *Realize it is hard for us to say no.* Know that your child and his wife probably have trouble saying no to you. I know that my in-laws love their son and want to see him; I also realize exactly how much of my happiness is a result of their parenting abilities. It's to my in-laws' credit that my husband learned to read, that he always wears a shirt to the table, and that he likes smart women. It would be hard to say no if Brad's parents offered to visit us the week before he deployed or after he came home from overseas.

6. *Encourage the young family to live simply.* The month before deployment should be lived as simply as possible. No big projects, no big expenses, no complicated trips. This is a period that ought to be lived as normally as possible. Encourage them to use the month before the deployment for tying up loose ends, taking the kids out for ice cream, going to bed early.

7. *Keep in contact with the spouse at home, as well as with your own child.* When the ship actually deploys, one of the best things you can do to help your service member is to support the family at home. Offer to attend some of the events during which his absence will be felt the most: dance recitals, ball games, trick-or-treating at Halloween. Also, make an extra fuss over the at-home spouse on Mother's Day (or Father's Day) and on their birthday; both are especially hard days during deployment.

8. *Be a patient listener.* It's tough to have sole responsibility for the kids when the service member is deployed—especially with a first

baby. Offer a supportive, adult ear for the spouse at home. Understand that after Homecoming, these calls will taper off—okay, cease, as if your child and his spouse had dropped off the face of the earth. In this case, know that no news is good news.

9. *Resist the urge (and the invitation) to attend Homecoming.* Although Homecoming is a big, exciting event—sometimes a once-in-a-lifetime event—it is also a private event. Hopefully, you got the chance to witness it before your child got married. Inviting yourself to Homecoming—especially if the young couple has no children—is rather like inviting yourself on their honeymoon. Homecoming is a time for the relationship between the couple and their children to renew itself. Visit a few days later and share the joy.

10. *Check out the Tiger Cruise.* If you really want to get in on the excitement of a Navy Homecoming, check to see if your ship offers a Tiger Cruise. This is an opportunity for parents and children (not spouses) of sailors to join the ship a day or two before she returns to her home port, and then ride the ship home. This way, you get to spend some time with your son or daughter, experience Homecoming, and then leave the young family on its own to get reacquainted by nightfall.

Being a mother-in-law or a father-in-law is never easy, and military life adds even more challenges. But I think you are up to it. After all, didn't you raise an outstanding member of our armed services?

Siblings

Most adults have trouble of one kind or another with their families of origin. I've got three brothers and a sister. You can just imagine the bones to pick, battles to refight, baggage to lug from year to year. I'm sure the way we play Monopoly or Hearts or Encore would give a Jungian scholar enough work to fill a lifetime. It makes for interesting holidays.

We all have the military in common. My three brothers all entered the military after high school—one enlisted, one went into ROTC, one went via a service academy. Even my sister, Mary, the family rebel, married a ponytail-wearin' Harley rider who was formerly enlisted in the Air Force. Like I said, we're a very strange family.

Thankfully, the military provided the geographic space we all needed to grow up. This was most evident when I told my friends I was driving fifty-six hours to Nebraska with my kids and my sister to attend my brother Steve's wedding.

They were appalled. "Fifty-six hours in a minivan without a VCR?" they cried. "Fifty-six hours with kids on caffeine? Fifty-six hours of nothing but fields of corn by the side of the road?!!"

At the time, I laughed madly, feet planted firmly, arms akimbo, certain that I, Wonder Mother, would conquer all via the economy-sized bottle of Benadryl in my purse.

But what my friends failed to understand was that the cranky kids and the endless corn and the Benadryl overdose were not the truly dangerous elements of that adventure. Did they not hear me say that I was traveling fifty-six hours in an enclosed vehicle *with my sister?*

Now, I know the experts say the closest relationship between siblings is the relationship between two sisters. But I still bear a scar on the inside of my forearm the exact size and shape of my sister's fingernail from our last cross-country trip in 1979. My sister thinks I got what I deserved for cutting up her photo of the Bay City Rollers. I think I should have gotten stitches.

It isn't really my fault that we haven't gotten along very well over the past thirty years.

I came into the world a loving and giving child, ready to grow into my role as one of the Hanes sisters in *White Christmas.* My sister and I were meant to dance around in blue organza gowns, double-date with Bing Crosby and Danny Kaye, urge each other to jump out of our Hollywood beds and get some buttermilk.

My sister had other plans. When I wanted to hear three little words from her, she thought they were, "Don't bother me." She could flay the skin from my arms with the tone of her voice. I was the termite problem she could not keep out of her room. The fly buzzing in her ear when she wanted to think. The rat in her dresser borrowing clothes she didn't even know she owned.

We fought every single day of our childhood and things never got any better. Our mother grew haggard reminding us, "Friends disappear, but siblings are forever!" Not if we could help it.

Then my sister moved out and there was silence—not adult friendship and certainly not any offers of blue organza gowns. But just before my wedding, Mary declared an armed truce. "Look, we'll never be friends," she said, "but we'll always be sisters."

Sisters. Fair enough. When I saw books about sisters or photo essays on the closeness of sisters, I never thought of Mary. I did not have that kind of sister. For the next ten years, we sent birthday and Christmas cards, never called, and saw each other only at our parents' house. I didn't think things would ever change.

When Mary turned thirty-eight, she and her husband visited us for the first time. They cheerfully sat through a six-hour swim meet. Then she called me a couple of times. We hosted our parents' fortieth anniversary party together back in Ohio. So when Steve and Stacy decided to get married in Omaha, my first thought was to invite Mary and her husband to drive with us.

We sat together in my minivan, not twelve and sixteen years old anymore, but thirty-five and thirty-nine. While everyone else slept, we drove in and out of rain, watched the landscape get steadily steeper, admired tumbled farm buildings and stiff white houses scattered on a landscape that rolled and billowed. Agreed we could live here. Talked for hours about everything—just like real sisters.

I've read that the relationships we have with our siblings are the longest-lasting ones we will have in our lives. They not only know us before we ever meet our spouses, they are our contemporaries. They lived where we lived, had the same parents, attended the same schools. They listened to the same music, wore the same clothes, used the same vocabulary, watched the same Captain Kirk on TV.

It makes you wonder if sometimes those same siblings—even the ones we thought we could never get along with—might be ready for a change at the same time we are. Shoot, if my sister and I keep going in this same direction, we figure that by the time we're seventy, we'll be spending the night at each other's houses, whispering secrets, and doing

Take Stock of Visits

Only you know your own family dynamics. Instead of spending the eight-hour return journey enumerating the many ways your family deserves to be committed to a federally funded institution, try to do a Lessons Learned. What went well? A hike, dinner out, or nine hours of watching the golf match on TV? What would make things better? More time, less time, or longer spaces between visits? Families aren't static. They can and do change. There's no reason they can't change for the better.

each other's hair. Wonder if the nursing home is ready for the invasion of the Hanes sisters?

Extended Family

Family friend Caran McKee claims that the world can be divided into Vigil Keepers and Non–Vigil Keepers—a distinction she learned when her father had an accident that left him in the hospital for months.

Caran says Vigil Keepers are the kind of people who visit you in the hospital even if it's gross or scary or inconvenient for them. They remember to send cards to high school seniors at graduation time. They attend big wedding anniversaries even if the drive or the flight lasts longer than the actual event. They travel for family weddings and funerals. They'll attend a local funeral even if they aren't blood relatives of the deceased, even if it's only to provide comfort to a friend or swell the size of the crowd.

For the true Vigil Keeper—especially the military variety—time and distance are no excuse. Although money (and getting leave from the command) can be a bit of a problem.

It's an interesting theory. Since Caran told me about it, I've noticed that Vigil Keepers tend to be evenly distributed in families, a few to each bloodline. You can always count on Grandma to come through. Or Aunt Pam or Cousin Michael or me.

As a military family stationed far away from home, we naturally miss all the events that keep geographically close families in touch with each other. We miss Mother's Day and Father's Day. We give July Fourth family picnics a miss. We never just happen to see our parents at church; we don't run into them at Target. We don't drop by.

But that lack of frequent contact doesn't mean we don't love our extended families. Or want to be part of them. It only means we have to be more vigilant than most about taking part in important events.

Thus, we tend to be Vigil Keepers. People who are greeted at family events with pleasure, certainly. But also with surprise. Other participants will say aloud, "I can't believe you traveled all this way just for this!" As if this family were not quite worth such a long trip.

We think it is. We think family is more important than a visit to the beach or a trip to Disney World. Not that you have to skip all other vacations, but boring old family has to be your Most Desired Destination some of the time. Because if you want to hold your place in your extended family, if you want your children to have a place, you must sometimes go there and occupy it in person. Bring a camera.

Friends

Find 'Em, Make 'Em,
Keep 'Em Forever

> *In the very serious search for fun people, these*
> *are some things to watch for: a good appetite,*
> *interesting work, good storytelling, slightly twisted*
> *sense of humor, fresh insight, brave choices.*
> —Karol Jackowski, *Ten Fun Things to Do Before You Die*

BY THEIR MOST RECENT CALCULATIONS, my friends have determined that it takes at least thirty-seven adults to replace my one deployed husband. They assure me that this number does not begin to assuage my physical needs or lawn-mowing requirements.

I think my friends spend too much time on extraneous calculations.

But they're right. Without my friends calling me and encouraging me and chastising me and picking up my kid at soccer during deployment, I would not begin to be able to live, breathe, or speak in complete sentences.

Is it any wonder I'm constantly crowing to military spouses that the one thing sure to get you through a military lifetime is the company and support of some Really Great Friends?

When I rashly mentioned this caboodle of friends in a column, I got a letter from a young military wife who was curious about how all this friendship making is done, once your school days are behind you. Like so many of us, this reader liked her coworkers. But those women weren't ideal for deep friendships. When they wanted to leave work and hit the bars, she wanted—and needed—to get home to her toddler daughter. "My husband is deployed," she said. "I don't know anyone from the command. My apartment complex doesn't have a lot of moms and kids. I'm not a local."

This woman wasn't whining about her life. She honestly wanted to know: How do you make friends when you are an adult?

Good question. Especially if you are a military spouse. Adult friendships are harder to put together than the ones we made as kids. Adding the rigors of military life to the mix makes everything that much more difficult. But it doesn't have to be a friendship stopper. Military folks often sustain the longest and deepest of friendships despite the distance of time, space, and the entire Pacific Ocean between them.

The hard-core friendship makers among us believe that in military life, you don't just make friends. By heaven, you earn them. Here are some of the ways we make new friends and embrace the old.

1. *Speak to strangers.* In all of those books about Finding Your One True Love, authors recommend you talk to strangers everywhere—in line at the 7-Eleven, in front of the deli counter, in the nuts-and-bolts section of the local Home Depot. The same holds true for making platonic friends. Start talking to the other mom-looking people at the pediatrician's office. Strike up a conversation at the local playground. Smile and wave at the woman in your apartment complex who is also struggling with the groceries and the car seat at the same time. Some moms claim they've made their best friends after running into them a few times at a McDonald's Play Place on rainy days. The point is, you aren't going to meet anyone new while you're sitting in your house. Find out where the moms and kids are and go there.

2. *Attend command functions.* I know you're sick of this suggestion, so I'm getting it out of the way early. Attend all of the department parties, ship picnics, children's parties, support group meetings, and Hails and Farewells that you can. Personally, I'm shy. At least, I feel shy and stupid and occasionally diminished at these events. Sometimes I show up only to realize I know *none* of the several hundred people standing around. If I cling to my shop-talking husband all night, I will surely pass out from terminal boredom. So I go talk to someone who looks even more all-by-herself-ish than me.

3. *Join more communities.* The military certainly provides you one community and work gives you another. But two communities seem awfully skimpy. Find other communities to join. Sign up for the March-of-Dimes walk at work. Attend the harvest festival in your neighborhood. Join a church—but don't just go to services. Volunteer with one of the church organizations. It's a way to meet people you can stop and say hello to after services. You never know. The president of the altar guild might have a daughter-in-law just your age with a child at your child's preschool.

4. *Let your kids choose your friends.* I want my whole family to like your whole family but the odds against this kind of friendship are absolutely astronomical. One of the easiest ways to make friends is just to be friendly with the parents of the kids your kids like. When my son was in preschool, I found myself waiting outside every day with the same Marine wife. Our sons were best friends. Even though Melissa and I started out not having that much in common, shared playdates, picnics, field trips, and errands gave us lots of time to get to know each other. And to like what we found.

5. *Take a class.* Sure, you hear this deployment suggestion all the time. And for people who don't have kids, taking up yoga or Italian culture or Physics 101 is a great way to fill and enjoy empty hours. But when you have kids—whether you are working at home or on the job—it's hard to find child care every week at a

certain time. And that assumes that you actually want to turn your kid over to another babysitter. Many mothers get around this by choosing some kind of class where the presence of a child is required (Gymboree, Yoga for Baby and Me) or one that provides on-site child care (try Jazzercise). It's a great way to meet other moms and kids who also are looking for friendship.

6. *Make friends with your own sex.* Even if you were the kind of girl who liked hanging out with guys more than girls, now is the time to learn to appreciate your own sex. During a deployment, we are more vulnerable to an affair than we want to admit. Avoid it by not hanging out with that attractive (or semi-attractive or even passable) member of the opposite sex. Same holds true for you, guys. Sorry.

7. *Accept that it takes longer to make friends with the locals.* Sometimes you run into a group of locals you really like. And though they are friendly to you, you never seem to be in their inner circle. It's almost as if their limited spaces for friendships are already filled. Don't take it personally. If you are around long enough, you may still become the best of friends with the local folks. If not, locals know everyone and can be a great source of introductions. And always keep your eyes peeled for other newcomers, both military and civilian.

8. *Move near people you know.* This suggestion may not help you now, but keep it in mind for the future. If you're moving to a community where you already have a friend, try to live near her. You don't necessarily want to land in your friend's lap, but if you are within a ten- or fifteen-minute drive, your school, shopping, and sports networks will overlap. Not to mention she'll know where to find a pediatric dentist in your area.

9. *Always look kindly on other military people.* I'm always delighted to hear that new acquaintances are part of a military family. Even if I don't have a lot of other things in common with them, I consider them my brethren, my community, my family. If they aren't good friend material for me, I might be able to hook them up with someone else I know.

10. *Give it time.* Unlike friendships in the sandbox set, making friends as an adult takes time. Lots of time. If you meet a potential friend, make a date to go somewhere together. If it goes well, do it again. You never know whether this person will be the one you're calling years from now saying, "I like my new town and everything, but I wish I could meet someone who would be as good a friend as you." May you be that lucky.

Talk Small Without Feeling Like a Big Dork

I say the stupidest things to strangers. I ask stay-at-home moms if they work. I ask kids what their favorite subject is in school. I tell pregnant ladies they are huge. I don't touch their bellies, though. Never that. Everyone has their strengths.

I don't mean to be obnoxious. I just get so nervous when I'm meeting new people that I even glance down at my own nametag before introducing myself. I swear, instead of meeting new friends, I'd probably be better off hovering over the chip dip. But in military life you just can't do that. It looks so . . . so . . . *antisocial,* doesn't it?

Debra Fine, author of *The Fine Art of Small Talk,* offers lists of questions and icebreakers for people like me who feel awkward around strangers. One of her best lists offers twists on the usual openers. Instead of asking, "Are you married?" or "Do you have kids?" Fine says we should try, "Tell me about your family." That way, people can tell you about wives or kids or parents or siblings or whatever they consider their true family. Instead of "What do you do for a living?" or "Do you have a job?" Fine says you can say, "Tell me about your work." Which means you could hear about someone's job or volunteer project at church or success in teaching the youngest to tie his brother's shoes. Instead of, "How was your weekend?" you can lead with, "What was the best part of your weekend?" or "What went on for you this weekend?"

Just being ready and willing to make small talk is an important first step. Before attending a function, think about how you would answer those questions. Think of something you saw in the news or heard on the radio that might start an interesting conversation. Ask your spouse who will be attending so that you'll be able to come up with names to go with faces.

Being able to make small talk at parties or military functions is one of our best skills. The more you practice, the easier it gets. Even if you don't come by it naturally.

Concentric Circles

When my son was in fourth grade, a certain mom made a point of telling me that her son and the star of the basketball team played so well together "because they've been playing on the same team since kindergarten!"

She told me this at every game. I wasn't certain why. My kid wasn't taking over the star's place. He wasn't even assistant to the star. At the time, we were just grateful he could run down the court without knocking down his own teammates and skidding on their blood.

I had a feeling that this mother's color commentary was a barked warning to stay away from her inner circle of fourth-grade-mom friends. A circle to which I clearly did not belong. For inner circles and outer circles and no circles at all are the stuff of which female society is constructed. That's something we military spouses learn early.

In *Odd Girl Out: The Hidden Culture of Aggression in Girls,* Rachel Simmons described this phenomenon among middle schoolers precisely. "Male society is a totem pole. Boys climb to the top," writes Simmons. "But girl society is a series of concentric circles. You work your way in."

That's the way it works in all girl societies. Grade-school girls work their way through gelatinous circles. High-school girls meld from one circle to the next. Grown women push against cell walls that are semipermeable.

This isn't necessarily a bad thing. For a gender that tends and befriends when under stress, it makes sense to draw your companions into a circle of strength around you. If you stay in the same place for many years, this works to your advantage. You become part of a group at church or in the neighborhood. You trade pregnancy and nursing tips. You exchange info about teachers. You build long-term, bone-deep group knowledge that is reinforced by weekly playdates and trips with the traveling soccer team.

We military spouses envy that. By moving thirteen times in the past seventeen years, I have excluded myself from the innermost circles. The inner circle I belonged to when my own children were toddlers is now spread from Washington state to Connecticut to Okinawa, Japan. And as much as I still love my "baby-friends," there is no power without proximity. The circle simply does not intersect at enough points.

Even after leaving the military, friends report it has taken them years to work themselves into the concentric circles of their civilian communities. If they ever get in at all. That is part of the pain of military life, part of the sting of moving—you must withdraw from all of your inner and outer circles. You must stand on the outside of circles you can barely see.

I sometimes wonder if women who join the military are attracted to it because advancement comes by climbing the totem pole. You work your way up in a linear fashion. Compared to the complex, concentric circles that define the rest of a woman's life, that straight, upward line must be quite a relief.

The mom who used to sit next to me at basketball games thought of circles as instruments of exclusion. She wanted to keep everyone out who wasn't present at the very beginning. But I see my own circles of friendship as instruments of inclusion. I don't let myself mind that I'm not in the innermost of circles. Instead, my circles are huge, encompassing all who touch them, all who need them. Because, for me, the power lies in infinite numbers.

Gossip

When we gossip we are also praying, not only for them but for ourselves.
—Kathleen Norris, *The Holy Use of Gossip*

Gossip. I hate that word, don't you? It could not have been invented by a woman. Not with all of its implications of ugliness and cruelty and smallness of spirit. The word is apt for the spreading of untruths and semi-truths and unbridled criticism. But it doesn't define the way women speak with interest about other people, about their own friends. We don't have an adequate word for that.

And we do talk about each other in military life. We talk about relationships. We talk about the looming implications of events. It's what we do to feel closer to each other. It's what we do to make problems less secret and less scary. It's how we worry aloud.

In her book *Dakota: A Spiritual Geography,* poet and essayist Kathleen Norris explains how gossip works in a farming community so small that people recognize each other's cars. Norris doesn't accept the usual definition of gossip as something mean-spirited and damaging. Instead, she contends that talking about each other isn't pettiness. In a small community, it is used to show solidarity. It is morally instructive. It tells how people manage to cope with the worst that can happen to them and what happens when they fail to cope.

"Gossip, when done well, can be a holy thing," writes Norris. "It can strengthen communal bonds."

A holy thing. Is that what we are doing? When we talk about each other in the military community, we often tell each other about this wife who is having a hard time with her pregnancy. Or that friend who moved to D.C. but didn't take the trouble to meet anyone and now feels angry and lonely. Or that military neighbor's kid who moved to a new community during his sophomore year and turned up on the prom court. Who knew?

What We Cannot Say and Who We Can Say It To

It's easy to see how that kind of "gossip" helps us, encouraging us to reach out to the people we're talking about or the people we meet in similar situations. It teaches us and warns us. It often brings us together, in the same way that talking about movies, books, and television shows brings us together. These conversations reveal who we are, what we value, how we think. That can't be evil.

Yet, having said all of that, I think it's important to stress that there are two kinds of gossip in which we military wives should never indulge: (1) the unit's schedule, and (2) what's going on with the crew. Which is real nice, I know. First I say we can gossip, and then I say we can't gossip about the things that matter most.

During a deployment, we all want information. At home or deployed, we want power over our situation. But when it comes to departure dates, return dates, and exactly what is going on in the fantail, We Want to Know Now. However, we must remember that what we want to know, what we insist on knowing, may put another person or an entire unit in a compromising position. We're aware of that. And still we find ourselves passing on information without even thinking about the consequences. Even when we know better. We Have to Know.

We don't and we can't. Even if your husband is the commander of the battalion, even if your best friend works in a neighboring battalion and hears things at work, you are not getting cast-in-stone information. No one knows exactly when the unit is coming home. Because those guys at the top don't know. They aren't keeping secrets, they're just keeping their options open. They can't afford to keep changing the date, so they bat around options like birds in a cage—and let us know when the bird is plucked, roasted, and ready to serve.

That fact does not stop a command crazy-maker from spreading the word, though. Every command has at least one person who is sure he or she knows something you don't know. The command has been extended for a year. Someone is getting fired. A person in your husband's division was caught in a compromising position.

It makes the crazy-maker feel so powerful. It makes you feel worried and stupid. But it doesn't change facts. No one knows the command's schedule for certain. No one—not even someone on the actual ship—is privy to all the details. No one needs to hear even the suggestion of infidelity from another spouse. I mean that. Hear those things and remind yourself to keep that crazy-maker away from you.

But what do you do with all that anxiety, with that bursting need to talk about the ship? Can't you tell a friend in the same boat? Do you really have to keep it all in?

I don't. I can't. I also can't reveal anything I think I know about the ship. I can write it all down in a notebook. Sometimes that helps. Or I can just tell Jeanne. Jeanne and I have been friends since before my daughter was born. And Jeanne has the virtue of both owning a phone and living in Colorado. She is outside my circle. She knows none of the people I know. Yet people, all people, fascinate Jeanne. She is a student

---

Mean People Suck

It sure would be nice if people who were hurting would just cry a lot. We would notice sad, sobbing people among us and naturally go right up to comfort them. But hurt adults don't usually cry. They just get mean or mad—or both. We have plenty of mean people in the military. Some came that way, others got that way from being here. Be merciful. Be kind. And don't take them personally.

---

of human nature. She is interested in my master chief's wife and how mean the ombudsman was to me and how the ship isn't coming home until kingdom come. She has listened to how much I wish my husband would leave the military, and recalled how I said exactly the same thing the last time we moved. Jeanne always ends the conversation by reminding me how much Brad loves me and how lucky I am. The right kind of gossip has a place in the world. It serves a function. We only have to know where and when.

Long-Distance Friendship

The other mom at the playground fixed me with a steely eye. "Moving around so much must be *really hard on your kids.*" She spit the words out like teeth. Clearly, moving is an act on par with selling one's child to Calvin Klein for modeling purposes.

I shrugged and said nothing. Ordinarily, women like this crush me. After speaking to them, I am hounded by the idea that my husband and I are doomed to wander the frozen tundra on donkey-back for the rest of our days with our psychologically mangled children trailing in our wake, hurling invectives at us. And our donkey.

On that particular day, I was inoculated against public opinion by the joys of long-distance friendship. I had three thick envelopes sitting on my dining room table. Three envelopes that promised not only Christmas cards and family photos, but Christmas newsletters too.

Yeah, newsletters. Christmas newsletters may be a national joke—the kind of pompous, thoughtless, just-bought-a-new-mansion/Hummer/poolboy missive that no one wants to read. To military families, however, newsletters are a lifeline—the divine reminder that no matter how many times we move, no matter how many times our friends move, we are a vital part of a thriving community.

The people in my new neighborhood think community is based on geography. Theirs is. They carefully bought houses on family-friendly cul-de-sacs. They sit next to each other every year on the soccer sidelines. They take the same pew at church Sunday after Sunday. Which is a good thing.

But the sameness of place is a luxury military families just don't have. We have to base our community on history, not geography.

In our family, community starts with the guys my husband went to college with and their subsequent wives and children. Then we have my baby-friends—a group of women I knew in Monterey who all lived in the same housing, pushed their firstborns on the same swings, and delivered a second child within a year of each other. We have our friends from Japan, who crammed twenty-seven people into a tiny living room for Christmas dinner. Friends from our first, second, and third tours through Norfolk. Friends from schools and ships and soccer sidelines. It's a community bound together with Santa-printed wrapping paper and a scrawled "Come visit!"

Are our military family newsletters full of more heartfelt sentiments and invigorating dialogue than those of our civilian counterparts? Hardly. We've got the same news of wunderkinder who take piano and trombone, juggle, play lacrosse, dance, swim, win blue ribbons at the state fair, and get accepted into Harvard's Ultra Early Admission Program. We've got friends who vacationed in the Swiss Alps. Hey, we've got friends with pools.

Peer pressure is such a great mark of community, ain't it?

But most of us do manage to tell the whole story on one side of the page. We throw in a line about how sick we are of laundry and how the dog finally died after eating all those salami rolls at the party. The blessed among us include pictures of the kids and sometimes the whole family—pictures that hang on refrigerators all over the country so that party guests will say, "You know Kitty? I know Kitty! How do you know Kitty!?" And we always send along our new address.

They say there are only six degrees of separation between any two people in the civilian world. We military folk scoff at six degrees of separation. We let the rest of the world mock Christmas newsletters—and feel sorry for those who do. For they must know all the wrong people.

Friends Who Leave the Military

We all have long-distance friendships. But some friendships seem to be at a longer distance than usual—especially when friends leave the military. The move out isn't like any other move. It's more like the move of nineteenth-century immigrants leaving the Old Country and heading for the New World.

Take our friend who retired from the military after twenty years. When Mike decided to leave the village, we tried to talk him out of it. Everyone did. He was the one whose fields reaped the richest harvest. He seemed the one equipped to lead. He knew enough about the work to be truly useful.

But the New World beckoned with her Streets of Gold, her Unbridled Opportunity, her Strong Economy. Our friend wanted more for his daughters than our village could offer. It was time to make a new start.

For a year, his family got ready. They put in their letter, got their things together, sent missives to the New World in search of new jobs and new cities and new schools.

And one day, when everyone else was on vacation, they left. They didn't just leave one home and move to another in a different part of the village, they went what felt like an ocean away. When we returned from vacation, they weren't just missing; to us, they felt lost. Because when you leave the Old World—whether through divorce or retirement or even widowhood—you can never come back. We all know this. But it doesn't make it right. It doesn't make it feel good.

We in the Old Country try to wait patiently. We wait for letters and pictures and advertisements from the New World. We wait to hear our immigrants report that the New Worlders do not follow our traditions.

That they do not use our alphabetophile patterns of speech. That in the New World, post-military folk are not as instantly accepted.

Immigrants report it takes time—years—to develop the same kind of friendships that used to come instantly in the Old Country. They report that their first jobs are transitional—positions that help them define what they're not interested in rather than what they want to do for the rest of their careers.

These are the details of their crossing. But putting those details into words takes time—time enough to be settled. Time enough to think instead of react. So give these particular long-distance friendships the time they need. Give them time enough to get back in touch and—eventually —report that everything is going to be fine.

Connection to Community: The Broader Scope of Friendship

Neighbors

Although we belong to our military community and to our own little circle of girlfriends, we also end up with neighbors. We may not seek them out, but we get them just the same. Sometimes this works better than other times. I've had particularly good luck with three neighbors, coincidentally all named Bud.

During one visit, my mother pulled me aside to hiss, "I had no idea your Mr. Bud was so *young.*" She watched him furtively as he mowed his lawn. "I expected a much older man."

I knew that. Ever since she heard that her previous neighbor and my current one shared the same name, Mother had assumed that my Mr. Bud would be a more contemporary version of her Mr. Bud, the man who lived next door to us when my father was stationed in Thailand.

Her Mr. Bud was seventy-ish, bald, and as wrinkled as the boxer who always sat next to him on his porch. Her Mr. Bud used to take my little brother to McDonald's, chat with Mother about the weather, and walk us kids to school on dark mornings.

My mother took one look at my Mr. Bud and her brow furrowed. Because my Mr. Bud looked like Kurt Russell with better biceps.

"Mother, Mr. Bud is just a friend," I assured her, "a neighbor." That didn't stop her from worrying. She listened to Dr. Laura often enough to know that men and women who start out as "just friends" often turn into something more.

But Mr. Bud wasn't really my friend. "Friend" implies that you go places together, hang out in the living room, share confidences. Mr. Bud never came into our house.

So why was he so indispensable during Brad's sea tour?

Mr. Bud did all the things that define a good neighbor. He was the one who reminded me to change the oil in the lawn mower, warned me about thieves breaking into neighborhood garages, called me when my son was running down the street in nothing but his underpants.

Mr. Bud seemed to sense from the beginning that our whole family needed a neighbor. When he found out how frequently Brad was gone, he didn't give me that I-will-if-you-will look that would have worried and frightened me. Instead, he seemed truly concerned about our safety. He gave me a business card with his home phone number scrawled across the bottom. "I go to bed early," he told me, "but if you hear something and you're really scared, I'll come over."

I never called, but the thought of him (and his biceps) was comforting. In fact, everything about him was comforting. We stood outside and chatted about the weather, my kids, his girlfriend, and the station wagon's mysterious ailment.

Mr. Bud would look at my son playing with the hose in the driveway or riding his bike in his Batman cape and tell me that I was a terrific mother. He noticed my daughter's good manners and great imagination. He ignored the blare of a TV that was on for too many hours every day.

When Brad came home from deployment, Mr. Bud was still our family's best friend. Imperceptibly, he pulled away while our family got reacquainted. During that time, he mostly spoke to Brad over the hedge.

My mother once told me, "I don't think Mr. Bud ever forgave us when we moved." Like my mother's Mr. Bud, my Mr. Bud gave us much more than we had given him. And we moved before we could begin to pay him back.

After a rainy winter in the new place, we finally met our next-door neighbors. I was not surprised in the least to discover that our new next-door neighbor was named (what else?) Mr. Bud.

Like my old Mr. Bud, this one has a manicured lawn, pristine gutters, and a deep tan. He doesn't look like Kurt Russell, but he's doing pretty well for a guy who's seventy-ish, bald, and wrinkled. My mother loves him.

One time I heard his wife, Miss Dolly, calling to my husband over the fence. Brad turned off the mower.

"Well, Brad, I heard your dog barking late last night. Do you know what he was barking about?"

"Probably a squirrel," Brad said helpfully, "or a cat."

"My husband is out of town all week," Dolly said, a little quaver in her voice. "I've got all the security lights on, but I need to know what's going on in the neighborhood."

I half-expected Brad to brush her off and get back to his lawn, the bench he was painting, the pizza dough he had set to rise. But he didn't. The annoyance melted from his face.

"Miss Dolly, if you're worried, you can call me. My number is easy to remember. It's no big deal. I can be out my back door and over there in a few seconds."

Mr. Bud would be so proud. All three of them.

Commissary Friends

I know we're supposed to cherish all stages of babyhood. But baby Pete hit that annoying age when the evolutionary command to get up and walk had him stiffening his gams every time I wanted him to sit down in his high chair or car seat or Exersaucer. Which was not usually a problem—given enough WD-40.

It was a problem the morning he decided to pull this trick at the commissary. A crowd formed behind us as I tried to cram Pop-Up Boy into the grocery cart. Pete thrashed his head from side to side, squealing and grunting like rigor mortis itself was crawling up his legs. Just as the ID checker called for backup, this little old lady chucked Peter under the chin.

"What a little *darling*," she cooed. "What a sweetheart!"

Pete, the traitor, dissolved into flirtatious giggles. His legs slipped into the seat. The safety belt buckled of its own accord. Pete turned away from the lady and then back to make sure she was still paying attention to him. The word "cherubic" did not begin to describe.

"You're very lucky, dear," the lady called to me as she patted Pete's foot and passed into produce. "These years go by so fast."

I know, I know. That's why I shop the commissary, especially on weekdays. While weekends are a time for working families and active duty to fill the parking lot beyond capacity, on most weekday mornings the commissary is full of mommies like me, uniformed guys with carts full of soda (for what purpose we may never know), and plenty of retirees.

Retirees like the one who asked me, "How old is your boy?"

I looked up from where I was stuffing seventeen Granny Smiths into a bag. The man across from me was thin and wiry and old and small, the way pilots can get to be.

"Eight months," I told him, wondering where his wife was.

"Eight months? That's a big boy," he said, putting three apples into a bag and tying the top. "I have a boy just like that—but he's forty-seven."

We both smiled. Not at the high humor of the remark, perhaps, but at the expectedness of the answer. Of course his baby is forty-seven.

"It's your exclusive benefit," trilled the recorded announcement to the shoppers. "We never forget how you became a commissary shopper!"

Picking through green beans, a man in a windbreaker volunteered that he had a new grandchild in California, and asked me whether Dylan was a normal name for a boy. I assured him that all the best kindergartens are full of Dylans these days.

The man shook Pete's hand solemnly. "You two have a good day now." Pete chortled. He loves commissary guys and their wives. Me too.

They are living proof that there really will come a time when my husband's life won't be so consumed with the military. When deployment will be part of our long past. When travel will be something we always do together.

I can see there will be a time when we will do our shopping together on Tuesday mornings. I might like that; I might not. I might send my husband up to the base by himself to drink free coffee and read labels and

Online Groups

So if friendship is so darn complicated and difficult to attain, why go to all this trouble? Wouldn't it be better and easier to make military friends through online groups, where you can easily find like-minded people without even changing out of your jammies? No, because real people trump virtual people every time.

A friend who works on policy for the disabled says that instant messaging (IM) and chat rooms have been a great boon to the severely disabled, opening their worlds in ways previously unimaginable. Her rule is that IM and chat rooms need to expand the number of real people you know to be considered a good thing. That means you need to know these people's real names and see their real faces before you make the Internet connection. According to my friend, if virtual communication shrinks the number of real people you deal with on a daily basis, then it's bad.

I like that notion—especially for military families. Because the world is made up of real people, complex people, whose ideas and feelings can't always be expressed in a series of one-liners. IM removes a layer of intimacy between people. It's an easier method of communication because it is more distant. But easier does not mean better.

compare prices to his heart's content. If knowing that is not a gift of friendship, I don't know what is.

In the dairy section, we caught up with Pete's lady friend from the front door. "Do you see which of these are nonfat?" she asked us. "The print is so small." We talked about a visit from her grandchildren. She smiled wryly, admitting she'd forgotten how busy small children could be. "You'll wonder how you did it without his help, though," she said.

I know I'm supposed to be shopping the commissary to look for bargains. I know I'm supposed to snap up cereals and detergents and pounds of cheap butter. But truthfully, I don't. I shop retirees. As much as I am a bookmark in the story of their lives, they are the pleasure of skipping ahead to see how it all turns out in the end. And I never fail to think I am getting a marvelous bargain.

Fellow Travelers

I am not the kind of woman who reaches for other people's babies. I like babies well enough, but I'm more the type who waits for a kid to be able to hold up his end of the conversation before we get that close.

So I wasn't quite ready to learn another lesson in friendship when one-year-old Sarah was led sobbing into the Sunday school nursery. I fully expected one of the Certified Baby Reachers to snatch her up. Sarah was, after all, a prime target—a little pink confection of a child with the kind of picture-perfect coloring you see only on Miss America and Baby-Cry-A-Lot.

And this baby cried a *lot*. She bewailed her outcast state until the plate glass trembled. Remarkably, I picked her up, patting her back clumsily like I was searching for a snooze button. Even more remarkably, she stopped crying and relaxed against me, one hand curled between us.

"Is she asleep?" I whispered incredulously to one of the Baby Reachers.

"No, wide awake," she responded.

I walked the perimeter of the room, dipping my knees every time I went past the mirror to see blue eyes wide open. Would this child never sleep?

"That baby needs a nap from two to four," said one mother as I passed by.

"Maybe she doesn't get held enough at home," added another.

An instant picture of Sarah's mother came to mind. She had no lap. Extraordinarily pregnant, this volunteer teacher had reached the stage when your arms and legs begin to splay out from your body. From behind, she looked like she was staggering under the weight of a twenty-six-inch TV. It hurt to look at her.

We nursery ladies came to the consensus that this was her fourth child. That she shouldn't have taken this teaching thing on. That she was overheard snapping at her child. Spread Too Thin was the conclusion—a capital offense.

I eased into one of the kindergarten chairs and fell silent, hoping Sarah wouldn't cry. She shifted and cushioned her head on my breast. Her blue eyes drifted open and shut. Poor baby. Annoying mother.

"That family is military, like you, aren't they?" one mother asked in the sudden silence. "Army, I think."

All of a sudden, I felt like a perfect idiot. I know better than to criticize other mothers, especially other military mothers—whether or not I know them and like them. In our military lives, plans are always subject to sudden change. Orders are accelerated. Dads on shore tours spend all their time at the airport. Parents or siblings are hospitalized back home. Babies come.

When Sarah's mother agreed to teach that class, she wasn't even pregnant. And now she was doing what we all do: carrying the load. She was struggling; she was getting by.

And *we* were criticizing *her*?

I wonder why we mothers sometimes forget that we *all* need help from time to time on this unplannable path. I wish that we had taken care of Sarah that day without judgment. That we had realized what Sarah's mom had really needed—to pick up her baby from a roomful of friendly, understanding people.

How good it would be if we could figure out a way to lend her a few hours of sleep. To bring over an extra cup of patience. To dispose of a carton of annoyance for her the next time we came by. Even though we didn't know her well.

I looked down at Sarah and caught her blue eyes staring silently into my face, her limbs limp with fatigue. She only wanted someone to hold her for a while.

I have never been the kind of woman who reaches for other people's babies, other people's mommies, other people's friends. But that doesn't mean I can't start now.

9 Hard Times

THIS IS A CHAPTER I WISH I didn't have to write. This is a chapter I wish you didn't have to read. I wish I could draw a circle around you so you'd never be sad and never be lonely and never feel poor and never know anyone who died too young.

I can't do that. No one can. But I can offer you a way to think about the troubles that fall on every life. Because it isn't enough for military families to expect our troubles; we have to expect them, meet them, and handle them effectively. That takes skill, not talent.

Fortunately, military life provides many opportunities to build up those skills. Everything we've talked about so far—the moves, the deployments, the kids, the jobs—all of it is building your muscle so you'll be able to stand up under any burden. You can do this. You can lead your family through hard times. Here's how.

Five Steps for Coping with Loneliness

1. *List what won't work.* This is the easy part. List everything you've done in the past that does not dispel loneliness. Watching mindless TV, making serial phone calls to friends, spending money you don't have. Diddling in chat rooms inhabited by people your mother warned you about. Eating all the stuff in the fridge you conscientiously avoided during the day.

2. *Identify your most difficult times.* Discovering when you are likely to be at your worst is the first step toward prevention. Some people hate the long, empty evenings after work. Others are tortured by Friday and Saturday nights—date nights. Sunday afternoons get me—the geological age that drags between Sunday church and the Monday morning drive to school is enough to make anyone nutsy before their time.

3. *Complete a task.* Researchers find that we boost our self-esteem when we complete a long-deferred small task. This does not mean you should tackle the three hundred bridal thank-you notes you've been avoiding for five years. It does mean you should plan to clean out your silverware drawer the next time you feel terrible. Or pull everything out of the fridge and scrub it. Or read one chapter of your book-club book. This is one time to think very, very small. Engineer a small success.

4. *Keep your eye out for other folks in the same boat.* Making friends with other happily-married-but-alone women (not men!) helps. In my town, that

Loneliness

I bet if we looked at the root cause of our most serious military family problems—infidelity, drinking, overspending, divorce, weight gain, poor parenting—we'd find the same thing: loneliness.

Loneliness is part and parcel of military life, the way it is part and parcel of the modern world. We are lonely for our absent husbands, our families, our far-away friends. We even get lonely for a grocery store that stocks the Velveeta and Shake N Bake where we can find them.

We must learn to handle that loneliness because something about the military invariably plants young people where they are most apt to be lonely.

Just look at Kelly Flinn, the Air Force's first female B-52 pilot. Flinn, who was kicked out of the service for committing adultery, blamed her heavy drinking and subsequent affair on the boredom of Minot, North Dakota, and the Air Force's failure to provide anything to do. In her book, *Proud to Be: My Life, the Air Force, the Controversy,* Flinn writes, "The truth about Air Force social life in Minot is quite simple: Everybody was sleeping with everybody."

That was the sum total of her excuse.

This was the same woman who spent three weeks in survival training at the Air Force Academy. Those weeks must have made an impression on Flinn. In her book, she wrote eight pages about eating bugs and skinning rabbits, crouching to look like a rock, and the thousand and one things you can do with a parachute.

She admired a POW at the Hanoi Hilton for building a house in his head so perfectly that when he came home and actually built it, he found he had only seven more nails than he needed.

"Surviving a prisoner-of-war situation is very largely a question of reining in your mind," Flinn wrote. "Because it's all you can control. And that's no small thing. It can be the difference between life and death."

Kelly Flinn failed to see what most of us fail to see about certain periods of our lives. Minot, North Dakota, that quiet little town, was *her* Hanoi Hilton. Like many other service members and their spouses, Flinn was the prisoner of a frustrating, lonely situation that looked as

particular marital status is so prevalent it is almost normal. Trade babysitting, agree to take a class together, call.

5. *Understand that on some nights, you're beat.* Sometimes nothing you try to do will make that frustrated/angry/sad misery go away. Many an evening, I've caught myself flipping through fifty-seven channels. On my fifth (more like fifteenth) round, I stop myself. Acknowledge that this day cannot end soon enough, take a bath, and go to bed. Hog all the pillows. Tomorrow is another day.

Coping with being alone and being married at the same time is a knack, not a natural talent. And thanks to these remarkable military guys we married, we'll have lots of time to practice.

though it would stretch on for years. If she had been stripped and beaten and thrown in a bamboo cage, she would instantly have understood she had to engage her mind to prevent herself from going crazy. Instead, this bright and accomplished woman slipped into a routine of bars, drinking, and unwise relationships—the refuge of the weak.

She failed to engage her mind.

To live a meaningful life within the confines of the military, you must *learn* to control your impulses. You must *learn* to tolerate difficult circumstances. You must *learn* to rein in your mind so it works for you, not against you. And, often, you must learn those lessons while in the grip of loneliness.

Like many other small places, Minot, North Dakota, boasts a public library that stays open until 9:00 P.M. on weeknights. It has a bowling alley, hardware stores, churches, and nursing homes. Two dollars will buy you a directory of clubs and organizations. Kelly Flinn would have been better off reading biographies of every astronaut ever born, building a

Victorian mansion out of toothpicks on her kitchen table, or joining the local quilting club.

Boring? Quite possibly. But developing skills outside the pleasure center of the brain is part and parcel of breaking free. And so much better than the alternative.

Debt

Why does money always have to be such an issue for military families? We do get paid. We don't earn the highest wages, true. Some of our junior enlisted qualify for food stamps. Even at higher levels, our income is fixed until the next promotion—or until the spouse gets a better job. We're pretty much okay with that. Before we signed up, we all knew the government wasn't paying in solid gold doubloons.

What we may not have known was that the intensity of our lifestyle—stress, risk, wars, moves, separations—would compound the pay problem. Stress causes many Americans, not just military, to reach for a credit card to push away anxiety and unhappiness. We go out to eat and buy clothes we don't need. We find a way to afford CDs, DVDs, SUVs. Name your poison.

Military families are most likely to overspend during deployments and moves. In addition to the unexpected expenses that always come up, military families seem to spend when we get those inevitable cases of Deployment Guilt or Relocation Guilt. When we're feeling bad because of a military situation, we're more inclined to spend to make ourselves feel good, good, *good*. Then we "spend" the rest of the tour filling up the financial hole we dug with our loyal intentions.

A 2000 Virginia Tech study cited by Roger and Rebecca Merrill in their book *Life Matters: Creating a Dynamic Balance of Work, Family, Time, and Money* found that many military families were negatively affected by their financial behavior. In fact, 20 percent of the military people studied were so stressed by finances that their job productivity was negatively affected. In most of the civilian population, that number was more like 15 percent.

So how do we take care of our families in times of crisis, yet still be financially responsible?

The Merrills may have an answer for that—one uniquely suited to our way of life. Most financial advice is short and simple: spend less, invest more. But the Merrills add a third item to that list: practice fidelity.

Yes, fidelity. Just as we must be true to one another's body and soul, we also must be true to each other in the moment of financial crisis.

That's not advice we often hear when it comes to money. Count on and rely on each other? Don't yell at each other, fight with each other, or control each other? Rely on each other for planning, accountability, praise?

"There has to be something more powerful in your mind and heart than the moment," writes Rebecca Merrill. "The best way to express love is not to go into debt. It is to manage money wisely. In the moment of choice it is hard to see that sometimes."

But it is so worth trying. "The reason money is such a tender item is that is shows the reality of your values. It's measurable. Concrete. It's just there," says Roger Merrill. "It says that what I wanted at the moment was more important than what we agreed on. That's why it hurts so much."

Roger and Rebecca Merrill have put together this plan for military families to help us better manage our money. Give it a try.

1. *Determine your financial goals.* Sometimes we have been together for so long that we actually believe we know what our spouse is thinking—especially about money. The Merrills recommend that you sit down and play what they call "The Money Game." Each spouse should write down his or her five financial goals, putting each goal on a separate index card. The goals can be anything from getting out of debt, to buying a car that runs in cold weather, to starting a college fund, to buying a house with as many bathrooms as you have teenagers. Put the goals in order. Then share them with your spouse. No matter how well you know each other, I bet you'll be surprised.

2. *Create a financial constitution.* Using your money goals, you and your spouse should mutually agree on how your money ought to be spent. This will be your "financial constitution." Notice the word "mutually." If you don't agree on a goal, chances are you

won't end up reaching it. According to the Merrills' theory, if your constitution states you want to live within your means and only go into consumer debt for housing or education, that great sale on a new CD player will look a lot less attractive. Thinking about your constitution might be enough to hold you off—at least this time.

3. *Use your constitution as a primary navigational tool.* This is the step that ought to be highlighted, circled, arrowed, and set in 3-D print. No plan will work unless you follow it. You and your spouse need to meet *every week* for a few minutes to talk about money, keeping your goals constantly in front of you. Why every week? Why not on payday or once a month?

"When you really connect with the constitution you feel great, top of the world, committed," says Rebecca Merrill. "But by the second week, things start coming at you. Stress mounts and you lose the vision." If you meet every week, you are either close to the vision from the beginning of the week, or near the accountability phase at the end of the week. It keeps you honest.

4. *Keep it up even when you are apart.* This meeting thing may work fine when everyone is at home and in port. But in our family, it seems like a month does not go by when my husband isn't at sea or on a trip. And during a move? I can't find my checkbook, much less tell you how much is in it. So, can't we skip the meeting while he's gone? In a word: No. This is the most powerful time of the financial constitution. Write an e-mail, send a letter, call on the phone. But do tell your spouse all about your successes, your struggles, your slips, and do tell him at the same time every week. The person abroad can give you feedback, even if it's just a couple of sentences. "It is a way of saying we're still together even though we're apart," says Rebecca Merrill.

5. *Look ahead to high-pressure situations.* Once you've been in the military a few years, you realize that certain situations prompt big spending. We've already talked out deployment and moving. But there are lots of other times when we overspend—even a promotion has a way of making you think you have more money

than you do. No one thinks it is fun to save money for things you don't want to have happen; but it's a lot less fun to pay interest on those things. This step is profound. We're not always able to manage it, but we try. Managing money is like losing weight. You never really conquer it. You never really give up.

"One of the very positive things about getting out of debt together is that it can strengthen your marriage. It reaffirms commitment to each other," says Roger Merrill. "You're not going to get out of debt in two weeks. But you can change course and take pleasure in being on a new road."

Childbirth from Opposite Ends of the Earth

I was so wicked tough the whole time. Didn't swoon with contractions. Didn't have a fit when I had to have a C-section. Didn't cry when I called my deployed husband, rejoicing that all seven pounds, seven ounces, nineteen-and-a-half inches of Peter Bradley had been born.

So *wicked* tough.

But I completely fell apart the next day when my hospital roommate's husband—a twenty-year-old sailor—strode up and down the room toting his newborn like a football. Kissed his wife on the other side of the curtain. Whispered how brave she was; how beautiful.

Then I sobbed. Quietly, so quietly.

Although I talk a good game, I've had a lot of wimpy moments in my seventeen years of Navy Wifehood. And frankly, this delivering-a-baby-while-the-ship-is-at-sea thing didn't bring out the Oprah in me. But I knew that before I went into it. My husband's first captain stoutly informed each and every new wife that he had missed the births of all three of his own children. He'd routinely declare, "There is an old Navy saying that the sailor has to be there for the laying of the keel, but not the launching of the ship." Then he would laugh as though possessed.

And we'd resolve to start using two, no, *three* forms of birth control. At once.

That worked. Our first two kids were born with their dad swooning at my side. Baby Pete wasn't quite so lucky. Although dads are sometimes sent home from deployment in time for the birth, most don't make it. At every Homecoming, a baby shows up to collect the daddy he has never seen. When the aircraft carriers come home, it's not uncommon for dozens of new babies to be waiting on the pier.

It would be lovely if we could get every new father home in time to tote his baby around the hospital room. But getting Dad back in time for childbirth is like lining up the tumblers on the locks at Fort Knox with a broken safety pin covered in peanut butter. It all depends on where the unit is, how close they are to the beginning or end of the deployment, how vital the dad's role is in the command, the amount of danger mother and baby are in, the state of war, the kindness of chiefs and sergeants and commanding officers, which school the dad is attending, and which transfer dates need to be changed.

The babies themselves complicate things further by regularly showing up two weeks before or two weeks after their due dates. Frankly, it takes an Act of God to get that guy home in time for childbirth—an event for which even USAA will not insure you.

Like most other Acts of God, deployment childbirth dredges up a wellspring of opinions on every military base. I've heard families complain when a new dad isn't allowed to leave the deployment for a birth—especially when his female counterpart left the ship after her first trimester. I've heard bosses complain that they are undermanned already and that sailors or Marines have no business having babies during a sea tour—much less going home. I've heard pregnant women cry that they absolutely *can't* and *won't* give birth unless their husbands are right there.

We aren't a bunch of hard-hearted idiots. Yes, we feel lucky to be having a baby. But when we have that baby alone, we feel the loss for ourselves as moms and our husbands as dads. And we especially feel the loss for the baby. The day a baby is born ought to be the happiest day of our lives—instead it is marked by the father's absence. Not fair.

At the time you give birth alone, pride carries you through. Thank God for that. Your assurances that everything-is-fine-please-come-home-ASAP sustain your family. But that isn't the only emotion you feel. Heavens, woman, you are still hormonal—you think you are going to get over this in five minutes?!! Doubtful.

For me, it wasn't until after my husband came home that I felt mad—or let myself feel mad. Isn't that strange? I felt that Pete had been cheated out of his rightful happiest-day-of-his-mom's-life status. And, truthfully, I felt that way for a long time. Months. Lots of mothers do. The babies seem to grow up and take this deployed-at-birth status as a bragging point—as though they were born in dangerous and exciting times and we are lucky to have the honor and privilege of their presence at all.

I can assure you that our disappointed feelings do fade. Think of them as another part of the childbirth experience—the way other people feel about a cesarean, or using an epidural instead of the natural childbirth they had planned. Don't let it become part of the lexicon of Eternal Problems in Our Relationship. No father wants to be away when a baby is born. The dads who've had to do it say it was one of the loneliest times of their entire lives. They suffer plenty.

When a baby is a few months old, it is understandable that the birth weighs heavily. It's the only thing that has ever happened to that baby. But as the months go by, the importance of the birth itself fades with your stretch marks. Other things become more important. And happiest-day-of-my-life status is given over to days like Homecoming or baptism or the Thursday He Finally Slept Through The Night. Brad and I are so lucky to have our Sweet Pete. And so lucky to be together.

Infertility

Keep busy.

That's all you get. Just those two words: Keep busy. Like that's enough to fill six, seven, eight months. A year.

Keep busy and the deployment will just fly by. Go to work, go to school, take the kids to the park, take the kids to the movies. Go visit your sister in Peoria. Just keep busy.

But what do you do when you have job enough and school enough, and your only wish is to have those kids to fill the days and hours? What do you do when the deployment puts the brakes on baby making—again?

What do you do when you reach the final skirmish in the infertility wars and you know you'll never hold a baby swaddled against the sea-sharp breeze? Never have a little boy in a mini–flight suit? Never have a sullen teenager who is more interested in meeting fine young Marines at Homecoming than boring ol' Dad?

What do you do then?

Maybe you just get in the car and drive. Drive until you understand exactly what is going on. Drive until you know what to do next. Drive as therapy, drive as prayer.

That's what Kristin Henderson did when her Marine chaplain husband deployed to Afghanistan following 9/11. She piled her German shepherd into her cool, yet elderly, Corvette and went for a cross-country drive. It wasn't the act of a desperate woman. It was a long-held dream, a long-desired plan.

In her book *Driving by Moonlight: A Journey through Love, War, and Infertility,* Kristin Henderson tells the story of her drive about. She tells how she and her husband, Frank, battled their infertility from Clomid to in vitro. When Frank was called up to go to Afghanistan, the infertility war ended—not because of the deployment, but because, for them, it was time for it to end. They were through; they had done all they could. They tried their best. They declared a truce. No more.

But Kristin and Frank found what many infertile couples find—nothing is over just because you say it is over. Nothing is over because you wish it were over. Experts in the art of war say that the winners are not the ones who get to say when the war is over. That honor falls to the losers. The losers must accept defeat before any war ends. It's a question of dignity.

When Kristin drove cross-country, she used the time to start working through the second part of her war on infertility. The longer part of war—reconstruction. She was a woman who could drive across country in a 'vette because she didn't have to worry about a car seat. She could drive by moonlight or midnight or dawn's early light because no one was crying in the backseat. She had the kind of freedom military wives crave. She had the kind of freedom we dread.

We don't discuss infertility in the military very much. We tend to be a remarkably young, and therefore remarkably fertile (sometimes overly fertile), group. Babies abound at every military event. So we never know what to say when we look up long enough to notice that nice couple and wonder why such nice people don't have kids. Why aren't they parents?

We don't have the words. Or we do have words, but they're always the wrong ones. Maybe all we need to know about couples who are trying to have children is that they are engaged in a battle, not a joyride. A battle that largely takes place underground.

The battle eventually ends, one way or another. There is—joyfully, thankfully, blessedly—a baby or an adoption. Or nieces and nephews, volunteerism, a big dog, an old Corvette. Or capitulation. Or acceptance. Or sometimes a little of each.

However it ends, it is a journey largely taken by moonlight.

Christmas: The Tao of Rudolph

I spent the better part of my childhood cowering behind my father's red and green houndstooth armchair waiting for the Abominable Snowman to just go away. Although I loved watching *Rudolph the Red-Nosed Reindeer* on TV, the Abominable's big blue lips scared me senseless. Brrrrr!

Maybe it was a premonition.

Now that I am a parent and have watched the show until I can recite large sections by heart, I realize the whole darn Rudolph fable is merely a metaphor for everyone's worst nightmare: Deployment Christmas!

Yes! That quintessential military experience that makes your Aunt Madge cluck, "I could never do what you do," until you want to throttle her. Now, by simply applying the Tao of Rudolph, you can finally explain away and triumph over the dread Deployment Christmas.

Foul Weather May Postpone Christmas!

It will never happen—despite the dire predictions of spinning newspaper headlines. We in Christmas Town, aka your friendly neighborhood military base, have long accepted that even though every unit cannot be home on December 25, Christmas still has a nasty habit of turning up in all its glory. Even if you decide (as some do) not to buy presents, put up a tree, or go home to the ministrations of your dear family, it still rolls around relentlessly. Get out there and sing an elf song.

You'll Be a Normal Little Buck Like Everybody Else

I know you thought you were going to star in this drama as Clarice, the little doe with the red-spotted hair bow and the long eyelashes who thought Rudolph was cuuuuuute. Nuh-uh. In this out-to-sea-for-Christmas saga you get to be Rudolph himself. Even though it may feel like your sadness sticks out like a blinkin' beacon, expect to wear that little black patch on your red nose most of the time. Remember, it's that wonderful nose of yours that is going to save Christmas after all.

Hermie Doesn't Like to Make Toys

Hermie-the-Elf didn't want to make toys any more than your beloved wanted to slave in an office building, work airport security, or stick frozen burgers into the broiler at Burger King. He wanted to be a military man—which sometimes means holidays at sea. Don't make yourself miserable by comparing your spouse's job to anyone else's. Sure, your next-door neighbor is home shoveling snow, hanging strings of lights, and eating all the green-frosted sugar cookies, but our sailors, Marines, soldiers, airmen, and Coasties are out there working to build Peace On Earth. It's a big job. Someone's got to do it.

Whaddaya Say We Be Independent Together!

In my favorite scene of the entire show, Hermie and Rudolph meet in the snowbank and swear they don't need anybody—that they are in-de-pen-dent. They set off, deciding to be independent together, with no clue about what they are getting themselves into. Sound familiar? If this is your first Christmas without your spouse, especially if it also is your first deployment, realize this is the hardest one you'll have to do. Send plenty of small packages, letters, and e-mails to the ship. While we here at home might have a bit of a blue Christmas, never forget that the one at sea is Haze Gray and Under Way.

Yukon Cornelius Is Your Best Friend

Now that you're on the journey, look for an experienced someone to hang with, like ol' Yukon Cornelius. Yukon knows just what to do when the Abominable comes into view; he's not just hunting for silver and gold. Douse that nose and run! Friends and family are your lifeline; they want to help. Stick with the ones who realize Bumbles bounce.

Even Among Misfits, You're Misfits!

Even though so many of our service members are deployed at Christmas, there still seem to be an awful lot of other people's spouses around. Imagine. Now that your own spouse is gone, you'll suddenly begin to notice other fathers at the school parties and holiday dance recitals. You even see them carrying sleepy babies around the mall. It's a mystery as big as why that little doll is on the Island of Misfit Toys. Even though you might consider hiding out from all the holiday fun, make yourself go and do. King Moonraiser would be so proud.

We Can't Let That Monster Get Ahold of Them!

When the Abominable Snowman isn't chasing you down, don't be surprised if it is nibbling away at your kids. You may be having a warm and fuzzy time decorating the tree when one of your young ones suddenly breaks down, crying that she wants her daddy. Take the teeth right off the Abominable by letting the kid cry without trying to talk her out of it. Once a person has been heard and understood, you'll be looking at a mighty humble Bumble. He's nothing without his choppers.

You'll Go Down in History

If your spouse is deployed during the holidays, especially if he is at war, realize this is a season that will go down in history. You'll never forget where you were or what you did this Christmas. There are plenty of service members ashore who wish they were out there striking a blow for freedom.

There's Always Tomorrow

People in Christmas Town really do care about their military families. They'll worry about you. They'll ask you what your plans are. They'll invite you places. They'll get teary over the Christmas messages from the troops. Feel blessed by their interest.

And next year, when you and your loved ones get to spend the holiday together, make the most of it. Remember that someone else's husband or wife, father or mother, son or daughter is out there standing the watch for us all.

Fear

Let any tragedy happen to a military family while the service member is deployed and the Letters to the Editor run fast and furious. That young wife shouldn't have been trying to drive cross-country alone. That dad shouldn't have run out for beer when the kids were asleep. That mom shouldn't have been napping even if she had just given birth, had the flu, had been up all night, and had four other children.

All true, I'm sure. But when I read those letters, the smell of fear is so strong it makes me want to stuff the paper away in an outside receptacle. Because we're all afraid. We're all afraid of the things that could happen during deployment. I don't have to list them for you. You're a military person, your imagination is probably vivid enough to keep you up at night for three solid weeks. Or at least sleeping with the lights on.

We never talk about this fear with our spouses, though. It's as if talking about it will somehow make it happen. It is this fear, though, that fuels our arguments.

I often think of what happened one day during deployment when my kids were seven and three. I was running down the stairs, carrying two baskets of laundry. I was hurrying, Sam was crying, and Kelsey was late for school. I slipped, fell down the last eight or nine steps, and crashed into a wall.

I hurt my leg and limped all day. But I could have broken my neck. All I could think of was what would have happened to the kids if I had died. People do die at home. Would Kelsey have remembered to call 911? Would she have been able to open the dead bolt? Would Sam have gotten into the medicine cabinet? The knife drawer? When would anyone have noticed?

Part of what is so killing about a deployment is the knowledge that you are carrying the full responsibility for yourself and your children all the time. That you could mess it up so easily—fall in the shower, unscrew the wrong lightbulb, misjudge a left turn in front of a truck. The likelihood of those things occurring is next to nil, but it could happen. And I would be the one responsible. Responsible to my husband.

Service members say the fear is just as strong on their side of the water. They worry about what would happen if we couldn't handle things. They worry about not being able to get home to fix something that went wrong. They are well aware of sniper fire and malfunctioning aircraft and the awesome power of the ocean.

We fear what we cannot control. That is human nature. And if you can accept that there are fears you cannot solve, you're halfway there. My friends and I confess to each other that after we check the doors and windows a billion times, lock our cars, take a personal safety class, and employ every other safety device we can think of, we all take that one extra step: We make a plan.

If you really can't brush your fears aside as *highly improbable* (which they are), make a plan. Go ahead, do it. Make a mental plan of what you would do if the worst were to happen and you were to become the one accepting the folded flag. What would happen next—besides the shattering of your heart? My plan is simple. I'd finish the school year with the kids, then move back to live in my hometown—I'd need my family behind me. I'd send my kids to my old schools and buy my own little house. I might need to go back to school for a while. Maybe I'd get a gray cat. My husband is allergic to cats.

While it's not much protection against the worst tragedy I can imagine, it is a plan that brings peace and sleep. The thought of a gray cat sitting in my window is so improbable, it coaxes my anxieties back to a comatose state. Plan for the worst, hope for the best, and let your fears hibernate.

So much easier said than done.

Desperation

We are told over and over that if we get in trouble, if we get desperate, we should call the command because the military takes care of its own. Well, we do. The command feels a personal responsibility for everyone associated with it. If things go wrong, call your ombudsman, Lead Spouse, CO's or XO's wife. Call the Family Service Center or the head of your Family Readiness Group. They'll point you in the right direction.

Did you know that the civilian world also wants to be of assistance? Did you know that most libraries (especially central and county libraries) have an information desk with staff trained to find answers to all kinds of questions? Sure, they can find the capital of Zimbabwe for you. More importantly, they can also find answers to questions like: What do you do when the novelty of having twins has worn off? What kind of programs are available to find work? Which groups help military families deal with spousal abuse, child abuse, and sexual harassment? What should you do when your apartment manager still hasn't fixed your shower and it's been three days since you had hot water?

"We make connections for people," explained Pat Cook, an information services librarian at the Virginia Beach Public Library. "They think we're just books, but we have so much more."

The library's information staff can find out which agencies to call, how to find support groups, who offers help.

"Nobody is having an original problem," said Cook.

Not even military families. Be brave. Get help.

War

I simply want to tell you that there are some men in this world who were born to do our unpleasant jobs for us. Your father's one of them.
—Harper Lee, *To Kill a Mockingbird*

Scandal reigned in my girlfriend Lori's neighborhood when a few of the mothers decided that the playground should be a "Gun-Free Zone." No cowboy pistols, no plastic space guns, no thumbs and fingers locked and loaded. And no sticks!

In some communities, this may have been seen as normal, even a good idea. But the playground in question was located on the grounds of the U.S. Naval Academy.

Lori said that some of the moms thought the rule was an unenforceable drop in the bucket considering the fact that midshipmen were being trained to shoot real guns just blocks away. Isn't it hypocritical to forbid children to play war when their parents are in the military? Shouldn't we be honest about exactly what it is these parents do for a living? Shouldn't we know where the money comes from?

The prospect of real war, danger, and risk seemed far, far away from their sunny playground. Yet when wars begin, we military family members must confront what our husbands and wives do for a living.

Despite myriad collateral duties, their actual job is not to chip paint and sort mail. They aren't paid to plan the Marine Corps Birthday Ball. Their foremost concern is not developing plastic recycling programs, manufacturing jet noise, or performing as some kind of human laboratory for every social science experiment to come down the pike.

The people we married are professional warriors. Warriors! These average-looking, freckled, balding, sweet people. The guys with whom we share a sink, fold socks, and sign mortgage papers are paid (to loosely borrow a phrase from General George S. Patton) not to die for their country but to make the other guy die for *his* country. Our sailors, soldiers, airmen, Coasties, and Marines are paid and trained to wage war—swiftly, efficiently, and in the most deadly manner possible.

We know them. They are good at what they do. They are not playing with guns; their professionalism is not the issue. Ours is.

During the 1991 Persian Gulf War, some families of active duty members and reservists were shown on TV sobbing and saying it was unfair that their husbands and wives were being deployed. That they weren't ready. That they had been doing it only for the money, and they never expected a real war!

We could accept that. Sometime during the Cold War, we families got used to thinking of the military as just a job. We could be excused for assuming that no one would ever be called into a land war again.

We live in a different world today. Even our reservists were not surprised when they were called up for the 2003 War in Iraq. When civilians asked them why they risked everything to join the military, many responded by asking, "If not me, then who?"

Certainly, their families cried at the moment of departure. Even if their loved ones never saw any action and never were in any danger, it is no joke to be deployed for months at a time. War is serious. War is personal. No one knows that more than we military families.

During the War in Iraq and the nation building that has followed, many military families covered by the news media exhibited their own brand of professionalism. Some wished only that their loved ones would finish the job and come home before the baby was born. Some worried about their imprisoned or missing soldiers and Marines. Some grieved.

And we were so proud of them all. Because they did not allow themselves to be surprised; they knew what was on the line. They were as ready as they would ever be. They were tougher than they had ever been. They had no delusions—only great hopes. For as much as our service members are warriors, we count on them to be peacemakers too. And to come home. Soon. Because we have plenty of socks still left to fold—and our wild kids are still running around the playground with sticks.

Family Tragedy

At the beginning of the 2002 school year, Navy kid Philip Devine had to write an autobiographical essay for sixth grade. He wrote about how many times his pet lizards shed and how he had played video games ever since they were invented. He noted the number of people who lived in his Port Hueneme, California, neighborhood who did not have pets (three).

About his father, Phil Devine, young Philip wrote, "My dad is forty-one and has dark brown hair like me and he also has hazel eyes. He is a command master chief in the Navy, which is the highest rank you can go! His hobbies are camping, fishing, and building things out of wood."

Philip didn't say that his dad always put work in front of the family. Or fought with his mom in front of him. Or had so much accrued leave that he had to sell back fifty days and still had more than sixty days left on the books and another thirty days to use or lose that year. Maybe young Philip didn't notice. Maybe sixth graders don't put stuff like that in essays.

Instead, Philip finished up with how he'd been born in Scotland when his dad was stationed there, and how he'd seen the "small" river that runs through the Grand Canyon. His teacher gave him an A– and printed "Well written!" on the bottom of the page.

During any other year, the essay would have languished at the back of a tatty folder to be thrown away in June. Instead, Philip's essay was printed in the program for his memorial service.

Twelve-year-old Philip Devine was hit by a truck outside a gate at the Navy base while riding his bike home from school. He swerved off the sidewalk to avoid a lady with a shopping cart. Even though he wore a helmet, he suffered massive head injuries. He died at the hospital a short time later with his parents at his side.

And life simply does not get any worse than that.

By all accounts, Philip was a wonderful boy. His parents, Phil and Nancy, dealt with this tragedy with as much grace as they could muster.

"We are overwhelmed with the awesome support of the Navy family," Phil Devine said.

But Phil Devine wanted to get one message to that family: The money that Devine earned by selling his leave back to the Navy was used to pay for his son's funeral.

"I'm not on some kind of guilt trip with this," said Devine. He didn't think that by taking that leave he could somehow have saved his son's life. Even before his son died, Devine had already started taking leave, started spending time with his son and daughter, started shoring up his marriage. Even though he thought he was doing the right thing at the time, he thinks now he made mistakes in what he called his "balance plan." He thought he had more time.

In a letter to his battalion and to the Navy at large, Devine wrote, "I am not on a crusade to tell everyone 'screw the Navy' and put your family first. We cannot always do that in our line of work. We choose to sacrifice time with our family in order to protect freedom and democracy around the world for our country.

"I think Philip's message is this: Take every opportunity that you can to spend quality time with your family. It is tough to do in the Navy, but you've got to take the time to do it. Don't sell back leave if you don't have to."

Phil Devine's advice applies to every tragedy that may happen in our families—illness, divorce, death of a parent. We only have so much time.

In his final letter to his son, Phil Devine wrote a message many parents could have written. "I am sorry for being a part-time father. I am sorry for leaving you all those times. I am so sorry for not living up to all my promises and being the best dad I could be."

Devine wants his son to be proud of him—not just for being forty-one years old, being a command master chief, and building stuff with wood. Devine wants his son to be proud of the more balanced person he is trying to be.

Death in the Military Family

"I know you're probably in the middle of dinner," our friend from Colorado began, "but answer one question . . ."

"It isn't him," I interrupted, knowing what she was going to say before she said it. "It isn't his ship."

Like many of our neighbors, we fielded calls all day from friends and family nationwide when the USS *Cole* was attacked in 2000.

It's a strange thing. Our relatives call us (or our parents) every time something serious or sudden happens on a ship. The same way Army relatives call whenever U.S. troops are attacked. The way Air Force relatives worry when a plane or helicopter goes down.

"Will they send him over there now?"

"Will that change the deployment schedule?"

"Do you know anyone?"

"Thank God this won't affect you."

Won't affect you?

To the outside world, an attack or an accident on a military unit is an isolated incident. A shocking event to list alongside other casualties. They can't imagine anything like this affecting their families.

We can. We military families do imagine it. Not every time the ship goes out, surely. We are not so dramatic as all that. The days at sea are nothing. The weeks melt one into another. A monthlong field exercise is absorbed into a year, like thirty drops of water in a Hefty paper towel.

Why waste fear on that?

But a six-month deployment or a yearlong separation has a status of its own. In that length of time, things can—and will—happen. Most couples spend at least one night before the deployment fighting, and then crying over each other.

What if something happens? What if you aren't here when I come back? What about the children? What if you never come home?

We imagine these things even as we deliver him to the ship or the base or the airport. And when he comes home safely, we think how silly we were to have even worried.

Perhaps it's because of these worries that we so strongly identify with other military families. Even if we've never met him, we know that nineteen-year-old Marine whose face they keep flashing on *Good Morning America*. We know the girl with her hair parted in the middle—the one who loved fly-fishing. We know the guy who stood on the pier the

> **The Tragedy Assistance Program for Survivors, Inc. (TAPS)**
>
> If the worst happens and your husband dies on active duty, the best support will come from people who have already been where you are now. The Tragedy Assistance Program for Survivors, Inc. (TAPS) is the best in the business. TAPS is a national nonprofit organization whose strength lies in its national military survivor peer-support network. Twenty-four hours a day, TAPS offers grief counseling referrals, caseworker assistance, and crisis information free of charge. Call them at 1-800-959-TAPS (8277) or e-mail them at info@taps.org. You can also find them online at www.taps.org.

morning before deployment in a half-hour clench with his girlfriend. We know those young ones wandering the commissary looking for the Froot Loops.

Every soldier is our soldier. Every ship is our ship. Every loss is our loss.

You can't live this life without walking in one another's shoes. We know each other. We know that the family whose beloved is killed will never shed that layer of abject loss. They may hide it, share it, live with it. Wear it thin and close to the skin. But they never will lose that layer completely.

The fact that they will live with the loss forever is both shocking and awe inspiring. These families are not asked to die in the service of their country. Instead, they are asked to *live* for their country, to live *with* their loss.

That is not a job I would want. That is not a job anyone would want. We wives and children and parents don't volunteer for it. There is no recruiter for military widows, orphans, or mothers of dead soldiers. We would never sign up for that task; we never push our loved ones into that path.

Our military members do it for us. They don't mean to. When they join up, they think they are only risking their own lives. They have no idea that they are risking the rest of our lives as well. We risk a lifetime of standing up for the choices of our beloved.

It hardly seems fair to both lose them and also live without them, and still be asked—no, *required*—to carry the flag in perpetuity. Bless all of our people who must walk that path. Remember them always.

Joy

I'M NEVER "IN" WITH THE IN CROWD. No matter how many places we live, I never seem to be friends with the people who run the PTA and the pool board. I'm never buddies with the mommies in the best playgroups, carpools, or investment clubs. I never find out until too late which teacher assigns too much homework and which one not enough.

In my neighborhood, the In Crowd is perfectly nice to me, perfectly friendly—and I am perfectly unable to have more than a seven-minute conversation with any of them. When I take the kids to the pool, I stop by their umbrella to do the pretty, balancing my bag on my shoulder, my weight on one foot. Then I scurry away with relief.

I'm weird that way.

The other day, we timed our arrival at the pool perfectly, snagging a shady spot just as another group was leaving. I pulled the mail from my purse: the new Williams-Sonoma catalogue, another credit card offer, a note from my mother looking forward to our arrival next week.

A group of men my own age settled in the shade behind me—mostly In Crowd husbands. The president of the pool board sank into the chair on my left, chatting me up about the crabfest at the end of the month, winter swim, his family's vacation at Cape Hatteras.

Then he asked, "What about you? Are you guys going on vacation?"

"Just back to Ohio to visit family. But we've got a wedding in Indiana."

When he didn't look properly thrilled, astounded, and excited about six days in the heartland, I added, "It means a whole night in a hotel room. *By ourselves.*"

I paused a minute, truly blissful at the very idea. When the invitation to the black-tie wedding arrived, my mother had instantly offered to keep our two children and Brad's two toddler nephews, as well. The thought of swirly dancing dresses, Brad and Rob in dinner dress-whites, and the novelty of hotel rooms had caused a flurry of excited phone calls between my sister-in-law and me. We couldn't wait.

I looked up to find the group of husbands all staring.

"What?" I said, looking back at them. "Wouldn't you give anything to be *alone* in a hotel room with your wife?"

"Depends on whose wife she was," one guy said. The boys thought this was funny.

"No, really. You get all that time to yourselves to talk and stuff. You get to wake up without cartoons. You can stay up and . . ." My voice trailed off. They all looked at me strangely.

Finally, one of them spoke. "We ought to get *her* to talk to *our* wives."

"Yeah, maybe *we* ought to go out to sea once in a while," said another.

The other two grunted in assent. I sat for a moment, perplexed by their unmistakable boredom.

These men offered their families the things I wished for daily: togetherness, consistency, stability. They spoke kindly to their wives. They enthusiastically watched their kids on the diving board. Their lives stood in broad, straight, even lines that deluged their families in security as plentiful as the water in the deep end of the pool.

On the blind, wild path the military offers, our family is never certain when we'll receive our next cup of togetherness. Every drop is meant to be saved and sipped and savored because it may be the last for a very long time. Is this enough to guarantee a happy marriage? Of course not. But something about the military has convinced us that even a single night in a hotel room in a place as prosaic as Indiana is worth hoping for, planning for, driving six hundred miles in August for. Couldn't these people see that as clearly as I?

The following Saturday, our table at the wedding reception was dizzy with happiness, the giddy mood of both military couples infecting even Brad's great-aunts and great-uncles. We toasted the old folks' long and happy marriages, tapping our spoons on the glasses so the oldest bride and groom at our table would kiss. We drank champagne with white-haired ladies in zinnia-colored suits. We danced with abandon.

When the tables were cleared to the floral arrangements, and servers leaned tiredly against the walls, we headed for our hotel room. And, for a moment, I reflected that a night out with the Out Crowd—the ones who do without so often that they don't forget—would do the In Crowd a lot of good.

The One True Path to Military Happiness: Learn Not to Plan

I think I may have discovered why some people achieve great joy inside the military and some don't. I know you're expecting me to point to some kind of Dalai Lama philosophy, or at least a chemical additive. Actually, I think it boils down to one practical little thing: Don't plan stuff.

I learned this by accident one fall day when Brad was cruising through the fall schedule. "I'm not going to be able to drive Kelsey to swim that night," he told me.

"And why ever not?" I said, exasperated. "Remember, we'll be at sea that day," he replied. "And the day after. And the day after. And the day . . ."

I made my scrunchiest face.

"Come on, I told you," he insisted. "You said you were going to write it down on your calendar. Don't you remember?"

Well, yes. I vaguely remember him telling me that the ship would be going out to sea here, there, and everywhere. That "N-A-V-Y spells ocean" and all that other malarkey he usually spouts when presenting the ship's schedule. But write it down? On my precious one-inch-square calendar space? Nevah.

Military schedules are the kind of things I jot down on my short-term memory in disappearing ink. It isn't that I'm wallowing knee-deep in denial that he will go. Believe me, he'll go. It's just that I've finally learned that entrusting your plans to a military schedule is like entrusting your grown-up hips to pants made from a fiber strongly resembling Saran Wrap.

It's simply not a good idea.

This kind of wisdom and virtue does not come easily. When I was a bride, I used to outline each and every day Brad's ship would be at sea in heavy black marker, preparing to drench myself in crepe until his return. (Funny how this did not seem melodramatic to me at the time.)

Then the ship's schedule would change, so I would have to scribble out the black marks and add new ones. Then the schedule would change again, and I'd have to scribble out those scribbles and start over—preferably on a new calendar.

At the time, I suspected that the military was doing this to me on purpose—like they had some sort of plan to deface Impressionist paintings worldwide, one calendar at a time. So I foiled their cursed scheme by writing in dinky ink letters with artful arrows to mark the length of the cruise.

Although these marks were much easier to transform into decorative flowers and ribbons when the schedule changed, I was forced to move on to writing in pencil. After that, I just carried the schedule on a separate piece of paper tucked in my purse. And then I stopped.

"But how do you plan anything?" a military bride I know wailed.

Answer: You don't.

You don't plan anything. You don't plan vacations. You don't plan to attend far-away weddings. You don't plan for car repairs or operations or weeding and seeding the lawn on a certain day.

You don't plan these things *for him.* (Or, of course, for her.)

Plans are just plans. There is too much happenstance in this world for us to count on sticking with our plans. General George S. Patton said that one does not plan and then try to make circumstances fit those plans. Instead, one tries to make plans fit the circumstances.

This works well with military life. It means that I'll plan to drive the kids to a family reunion by myself if the unit doesn't make it back in time. It means I'll read up on refundable airline tickets before I buy. It means I will let go of any need I have to control the ship's schedule.

Brad popped his head back in the kitchen. "Oh, babe, did I tell you this? We're going to be out on your birthday again this year."

"No problem," I said, throwing my calendar onto the counter. "I'll make a note of it right here."

Final Instructions

I love *Life's Little Instruction Book* by H. Jackson Brown Sr. Originally written when his son went to college, that book and the series that followed (and books like them) came with advice like, "Never pass up an opportunity to hold your dad's hand," or "Dive for the bouquet," or, "Be careful whom you marry; 95 percent of your happiness and unhappiness will come from them."

"I read years ago that it was not the responsibility of the parent to pave the road for their children, but to provide a road map," writes Brown. We are the same way in the military. We cannot ease the path of every young person who joins us on our journey, but we can give them directions. Here are the ones I want you to have.

1. Put your marriage first. It is the center of the military family's happiness.

2. Send a care package with a sweatshirt, a pillowcase, or a bath towel that smells like home—not lube oil or desert dust.

3. Plant tulip bulbs, hydrangea bushes, and tomato plants even if you are scheduled to move before they bloom or ripen. The neighbors will never forget you and the new tenant will bless you always.

4. Get a smallish dog.

5. Don't discuss your husband's career. Your friends don't care. Your enemies don't believe you. Your shipmates know better.

6. When your spouse gets orders to another state, move there.

7. Take the kids to visit the in-laws even if your spouse can't go. It's the right thing to do.

8. Live in military housing at least once.

9. Know the difference between neighbors, friends, and shipmates. Share accordingly.

10. Never miss a family wedding or funeral. If you don't take your place in the extended family, you will lose it.

11. Don't watch the ship leave or the plane take off.

12. Never miss a Homecoming—even a little one.

13. When you move, leave a fresh box of Popsicles in the freezer for the new kids on the block.

14. Know the mailing address of your spouse's unit, which department he works in, the name of his boss, and at least three phone numbers where he can be reached.

15. Don't call your husband at work unless he owns the phone he is speaking on.

16. Don't move a high school senior. By the time a kid is eighteen, she has done enough for the military.

17. Attend some of the balls, most of the Hails and Farewells, none of the business meetings, and all of the retirement and change of command ceremonies.

18. Find out what an ombudsman does.

19. Visit the ship in a foreign port during deployment—without the kids.

20. When they play the national anthem and raise the flag, stand and cover your heart with your hand. Your children are watching.

21. Find a home church, mosque, or synagogue and attend regularly. God is a necessity.

22. Arrange your photo albums by address, not date. It makes pictures and memories easier to retrieve.

23. Tell your kids how much you admire them. Make a list of the things they have done: outwitted that bully in the fifth grade, tried out for football when the new school didn't have lacrosse, kept in touch with six friends.

24. Live overseas. Coming back to Wal-mart is as big an experience as doing without it.

25. Drive as far as you have to for a playdate. Eight hours is not too far. Best friends don't happen every day.

26. Don't lose yourself in your husband's identity. He fell in love with you, not a mirror.

27. Visit your family during deployment. They'll enjoy having you all to themselves for a change.

28. Develop adaptable job skills. You will move more than once.

29. Park in the back of the commissary parking lot. Make a retiree or a pregnant mom feel lucky today.

30. Know that when you have the least to give, your kids need you the most.

31. Remember the military wife motto: Semper Gumby—always flexible.

32. Be adaptable and confident. Stand up to him; bend to him. This life isn't for everyone. Not everyone can do it. Not everyone can do it for twenty or thirty years. I don't know that I can. The military way of life is never easy, but it certainly keeps things interesting.

What If I'm Wrong?

One Sunday last winter, I sent my husband off for two months. Frankly, I didn't send him, the Navy sent for him. I let him go.

As he loaded his car and hid his excitement, I sat and read the newspaper with my forehead balanced on my hand. I digested the steak and eggs he'd made us for breakfast.

Brad went upstairs to bid the babies good-bye, to hug them and kiss them and tell them to be good. I listened to his footsteps on the hardwood floors and the sounds of mingled voices.

He folded himself into his car, released the parking break, waved. I cried as he drove away from me. I cry every time. No matter how much philosophy I've got in my pocket, being left still hurts. What kind of joy is that?

During the looming of that long, rainy afternoon, I found myself wondering why I'm doing this. What if I'm wrong? I've spent this whole book trying to describe how to stay married to a military guy and how to build a happy, functional family. Yet, it still hurts. Maybe I would be better off spending my time writing columns and books about how to get out of the military.

Stultifying suburbia looks awfully good on a lonely Sunday afternoon.

But even as I wondered, a thought occurred to me: It may cost just as much sadness to live a small life as it does to live a big one. It may hurt just as much, just in different ways. Military spouses hurt from being left and from stretching to fill such a big role. Maybe our civilian counterparts hurt from squeezing themselves into a more constrained life. Maybe they long for travel. Maybe they catch themselves wishing for higher highs and lower lows. Maybe they wish they could move away from home.

I know the military is not the only place to live a big life. For me, it's the task at hand, it's what's on my plate—the way it is for everyone who marries a service member. Thankfully, we wives sit at a table with the kind of men who want to be in the military. Dutiful men, responsible men, men who will serve us as well as their country. This is our sorrow to sup. This is our joy to feast upon. I do so love a guy in uniform.

Although I don't know everything there is to know about being a military wife, I thank you for graciously reading what I have learned thus far. As my column readers constantly remind me, there is always something else I need to learn. Some other fear to conquer, some other angle from which I can look at things. Some joy I forgot to outline. Please visit my website at www.jaceyeckhart.com. Or drop me an e-mail at jacey@jaceyeckhart.com. You've read my story. I want to hear yours.

Acknowledgments

*No matter what accomplishments you achieve,
somebody helped you.* —Althea Gibson

MY FIRST THANKS GO TO the readers of the *Virginian-Pilot* in Norfolk, Virginia. Many of the essays in this book first appeared as columns in the pages of their morning paper from 1998–2004. These readers took the time to write me encouraging letters and e-mails. They shared their own military experiences. They called me to task when I was wrong and when I was whining. Most of all, they didn't mind when their local columnist didn't live locally. They buoyed me. And for that, I am truly grateful.

Many writers have writing groups to sustain them. I move too much to build that kind of professional trust. Instead, I am blessed with a family that stepped up to do the job. My husband, Brad, cuts through the writer's anxiety like no one else can. He encourages me daily and loves me completely. I don't deserve to be so lucky.

My mother, Judy Eckhart, was my first fan. My earliest memories are of her saying, "You are so creative!"

She read every word of my manuscript, helped define chapters, and didn't say a word about my spelling. All that I am and hope to be I owe to my mother.

My father, John Eckhart, is everything a husband, father, and military man ought to be. Raised in a small town, he set out to give his own children the breadth of the Atlantic Ocean, the heights of Glacier National Park, the length of I-75. And he succeeded.

My daughter, Kelsey, not only shared her personal experiences but also offered up countless hours of babysitting so this book might exist. Ask me how I do it and I'll tell you: I have Kelsey.

My son Sam is my fellow "P"-in-the-pod. He walks with me and says, "Tell me about your writing." Nothing better.

My son Peter not only keeps me company during school days, he's also my time manager. Thanks for all the long nap times.

I also would like to thank my siblings, Mary, Steve, Dan, and Nick, for keeping me from being way too dramatic throughout my military childhood. Thanks for making me sweat.

I would like to thank Larry and Judy, my parents-in-law, for supporting our family through all of our many moves and for raising the finest person I have ever known. No one has ever done a better job.

Thanks also go to Char Foley who put up with my bitter-little-military-wife stage and taught me how to get over it.

Barry Grote taught me to market the product and close the sale.

Earl Swift gave my first column a place to be printed and set down many of the guidelines I still use for writing.

Kay Addis mentored my column whenever necessary. Her notes mean the world to me.

My editors, Dianne Tennant, Latane Jones, and Michele Vernon-Chesley, and the staff of the *Virginian-Pilot* deserve many thanks from our military community. They truly understand the city in which we live and publish a very fine newspaper.

Thanks also go to all of the professionals at the Naval Institute Press. Thanks for caring about military families.

I would like to thank the many military families that have served with us and befriended us through the years. They convince me daily that men and women in uniform are a valuable resource worth serving and preserving. I especially would like to mention Ed and Dawn Delaney and their children, Eddie, Robert, and Anna, who are a font of ideas. Also Jim and Jeanne Halferty, Bob and Kim James, Ken and Lori McElroy, Bob and Kathy McKenna, Jeff and Melissa Peterson, and Rob and Karen Douglass.

Finally, I'd like to thank a stranger, Julia Cameron, whose books about creativity taught me to stop talking about writing and simply to write.

And to the crew of the Starbucks Broaddale Store in Falls Church, Virginia, thanks for the office space. Thanks for knowing my name.

Bibliography

Bateson, Catherine. *Composing a Life.* New York: Plume, 1989.

Brown, H. Jackson. *Life's Little Instruction Book.* Nashville: Rutledge Hill, 1991.

Brown, Margaret Wise. *Goodnight, Moon.* New York: Harper & Row, 1947.

Conroy, Pat. *The Great Santini.* New York: Houghton Mifflin, 1976.

Cunningham, Michael. *The Hours.* New York: Picador USA, 2000.

Eisenhower, Susan. *Mrs. Ike: Memories and Reflections on the Life of Mamie Eisenhower.* New York: Farrar, Straus, and Giroux, 1996.

Farley, Janet I. *Jobs and the Military Spouse: Married, Mobile, and Motivated for the New Job Market.* Manassas Park, VA: Impact Publications, 1997.

Fine, Debra. *The Fine Art of Small Talk: How to Start a Conversation, Keep It Going, Build Rapport, and Leave a Positive Impression.* Englewood, CO: CareerTrack Publications, 1997.

Flinn, Kelly. *Proud to Be: My Life, the Air Force, the Controversy.* New York: Random House, 1997.

Harrell, Margaret C. *Invisible Women: Junior Enlisted Army Wives.* Santa Monica: RAND, 2000.

Henderson, Kristin. *Driving by Moonlight: A Journey through Love, War, and Infertility.* New York: Seal, 2003.

Jackowski, Karol. *Ten Fun Things to Do Before You Die.* New York: Hyperion, 1989.

Manchester, William. *The Last Lion: Winston Spencer Churchill Alone 1932–1940*. Boston: Little, Brown, 1988.

McCain, John, and Mark Salter. *Faith of My Fathers: A Family Memoir*. New York: Random House, 1999.

Merrill, Roger and Rebecca Merrill. *Life Matters: Creating a Dynamic Balance of Work, Family, Time, and Money*. New York: McGraw-Hill, 2003.

Norris, Kathleen. *Dakota: A Spiritual Geography*. New York: Houghton Mifflin, 1993.

Pipher, Mary. *The Shelter of Each Other: Rebuilding Our Families*. New York: Grosset/Putnam, 1996.

Rilke, Rainer Maria. *Letters to a Young Poet*. Trans. Joan M. Burnham. Novato, CA: New World Library, 1992.

Simmons, Rachel. *Odd Girl Out: The Hidden Culture of Aggression in Girls*. New York: Harcourt, 2003.

Susanka, Sarah. *The Not So Big House: A Blueprint for the Way We Really Live*. Newtown, CT: Taunton Press, 1998.

Wertsch, Mary Edwards. *Military Brats: Legacies of Childhood Inside the Fortress*. New York: Harmony Books, 1991.

Yapko, Michael J. *Breaking the Patterns of Depression*. New York: Main Street, 1998.

About the Author

As an Air Force brat, Jacey Eckhart grew up swearing she would never enter the military herself or marry anyone who did. She thought she would love her own children too much to ever make them move. Jacey married the first Navy guy she dated. Seventeen years later, she and her husband have moved thirteen times, tackled five deployments, and raised three kids. Jacey has written more than four hundred columns for the *Virginian-Pilot* in Norfolk, Virginia, that encourage, empower, and entertain military families everywhere.